Politico's
Guide
To

Careers in Politics and Government

Sally
Gillman

First published in Great Britain 2001
Published by Politico's Publishing
8 Artillery Row
Westminster
London
SW1P 1RZ

Tel 020 7931 0090
Fax 020 7828 8111
Email publishing@politicos.co.uk
www.politicos.co.uk/publishing

A catalogue record of this book is available from the British Library.

ISBN 1 902301 30 7

Printed and bound in Great Britain by Creative Print and Design

Contents

	Acknowledgements	1
	Introduction	2
1	Politicians	4
2	Politicians' staff	18
Interview	Bruce Grocott	28
3	The staff of the Parliaments	35
4	Civil Service – General Fast Stream	71
5	Civil Service – Main Stream	102
Interview	Mike O'Connor CBE	118
6	Academia	127
7	Think-tanks and pressure groups	143
Interview	Iain Dale	151
8	Public Affairs (lobbying)	158
9	Political parties and trade unions	170
Interview	Greg Rosen	185
10	Journalism	189
Interview	Martin Bell OBE	201
11	And a few more . . . Market Research/Polling; Local Government and Quangos; Publishing; Teaching in Schools and Colleges	207
	Index	214

Acknowledgements

My sincere thanks to all the very busy people who gave their time so generously to talk to me and, very often, read over drafts of the work. Particular thanks are due to the Fast Streamers for their diaries.

Thanks also to my family, friends and my colleagues at Staffordshire University Careers Service for their moral and practical support. A special thank you goes to Caroline Harvey of Coventry University Careers Service, on whom I inflicted drafts of most of the chapters, and last but not least, my gratitude to Iain Dale of Politico's.

Needless to say any, errors or omissions are mine alone.

Sally Gillman

Introduction

The idea for this book came from my work as a university careers adviser talking to students who said: 'I'm interested in politics – what jobs are there?' Though not all the jobs covered actually require a degree, in practice most of the people doing them will be graduates. So, I hope this book will be of use to graduates, current undergraduates and those planning to go to university who are already thinking about a career in or around politics.

Why these particular jobs?

I admit that my definition of 'politics' is a rough-and-ready one. Basically, all the areas covered are in some way connected to domestic policy: its formulation and implementation, and/or the analysis and workings of the mainstream political process in general. At one end of the spectrum is an academic spending a lifetime studying and writing about political philosophy, at the other an executive officer in the Cabinet Office implementing the day-to-day process of organisational reform. In between are myriad individuals and organisations facilitating and influencing the political process.

For a number of reasons, not least one of space, I have chosen to concentrate on British-based and primarily British-focused employers and employment. Opportunities with international organisations and the European Union institutions are not covered – they could fill a book by themselves. (But, if you are interested in these areas, their websites are very good starting points for information – www.psr.keele.ac.uk has links to most of them.) Even within the domestic scene, I'm sure there are other jobs that could have been included, but I think, at least I hope, the book covers a pretty good range of opportunities. The one omission that you may notice is any reference to Northern Ireland. This is no slight, but as all politicians, their staff as well as officials, wrestle with the peace process, it struck me that they have far more important things on their minds than to answer my questions.

What is covered?

The bottom line is always that until you do a job, you can't know exactly what is involved, but I hope that the chapters will give you a good flavour of the work – at least enough to know if it's something you might want to find out more about. Wherever possible, I have quoted people doing the jobs – it's always better to get the information from source – and given information about their academic and work background. Not all of the jobs are open to new graduates, but with the inclusion of those that require some previous experience, you should be able to see possible career pathways. People do move between different types of job in politics as in other walks of life, and the interviews between the chapters demonstrate this. Each of the people interviewed has worked in a number of areas, and between them they cover just about the whole range in the book.

At the end of each chapter (except the last) or section are summary and further information sections. The former gives a précis of the main factual information. In areas of work where requirements and terms and conditions are laid down, then it is quite extensive. In others, particularly where the section covers a number of different jobs in different organisations, it is, of necessity, less specific. Only in one case did I think it would be pointless to try and summarise it at all, and that was for pressure groups, of which there are so many, each with very different roles and structures. The further information section is not meant to be a comprehensive reading list, but may mention a few books or websites that might be of use. However, I would also encourage you to look at the official higher education careers website, www.prospects.ac.uk, which is a mine of information on careers and courses. Also, if you are currently at university (or a graduate), do use the careers service, where there are many excellent publications produced by the Association of Graduate Careers Advisory Service (AGCAS), as well as useful reference books and, of course, helpful careers staff.

Good luck!

1   Politicians

For large sections of the British public, the general election of 2001 passed by, if not unnoticed, then uncared about. For these people, the roll-call of results in the papers the following day would be so many anonymous names and meaningless numbers. But behind those figures of votes cast and majorities gained lay weeks of organisation, millions of leaflets folded and labels stuck by countless volunteers, and a great deal of hope. Hundreds of candidates will have walked thousands of streets in every weather, braving the dogs (who make no distinction between politicians and postmen), knocking on doors and getting involved in arguments and debates – good-natured or bad-tempered – with pro, anti or indifferent voters. Then come the results; up and down the country, they stand on stages or makeshift podiums in countless clubs and sports halls, glowing with success or biting back the disappointment, and all in the public gaze. Why do they want to put themselves through this? What sort of people are MPs? And what do they actually do when they finally get those treasured letters after their name?

Why do they want to be a Westminster MP?

The reason most often cited is to work for their constituents. Paul Farrelly, a former journalist and Labour MP for Newcastle-under-Lyme elaborates:

I think you can help people at three different levels. Last year when I was canvassing in the local elections, I came across an old lady who'd waited five years for her windows to be painted. When the council finally did do the work, they painted them shut! So you go and make a complaint on her behalf to the local council. That's helping individuals. But then, on the second level, there are problems that affect groups of local people, health facilities for instance. Concerns like these can only be solved at a higher level, so you work with the local MPs. Lastly, there are those issues that can only be fought and won at the national level – like the minimum wage, for example. Throughout my life, I've helped people with industrial tribunals, employment cases, health appeals and so on. As a constituency MP, I will go on helping people like this, and be able to do even more.

In the run-up to the election, the *Guardian* asked sitting MPs to say what they were proudest of achieving since the 1997 election. Of the 231 who responded to the invitation, the majority mentioned helping individuals or groups of constituents by securing investment in health or education or improving conditions for employment opportunities. Many were also proud of their role in bringing about legislation that would have a positive effect on the lives of many people. David Amess, Conservative MP for Southend West, said, 'My proudest achievement was to pilot successfully through parliament the Warm Homes and Energy Conservation Act. This should improve the lives of up to five million people, taking them out of fuel poverty by ensuring their homes are properly insulated.' And Dr Vincent Cable, Liberal Democrat, Twickenham, saw his most important contribution as helping to persuade the government to introduce standards in the NHS which outlaw discrimination in health treatment on the basis of age. No doubt these worthy sentiments expressed by MPs are genuine, but it is unlikely that the desire to 'help people' is the only reason for wanting the job. For the rest of us, career choice involves all sorts of considerations – challenge, power, status, promotion prospects, money, choice of colleagues, values, enjoyment, etc. Why should MPs be any different? Given the uniqueness of Parliament and the nature of party politics, which is all about competing and power, surely the desire to be on the winning side, to be at the top of the tree and at the heart of public life with a chance of making great policy decisions (and possibly ending up in the history books), must figure in the rich mixture of motivations? For whatever reason, perhaps because it's just not seen as very British, politicians don't flaunt such motives. But read some political autobiographies and you will soon get the sense of intensity and exuberance with which they play the game – the plotting, the planning, the friendships and the enmities. Politics is undoubtedly worthy, but politicking is also fun!

What sort of people are they?

Well the standing joke, though true, was that MPs couldn't be lunatics or peers. In fact, those hereditary peers who are not members of the House of Lords (since the recent reform of that Chamber) may now stand. You must be a British citizen or a citizen of a Commonwealth country or the Republic of Ireland and cannot be an undischarged bankrupt, a prisoner currently serving a sentence of one year plus or a serving police officer, civil servant, judge or a member of the armed forces. You do not have to be resident in the constituency for which you are standing. The minimum age is 21.

In the current parliament there are 541 men, 118 women, a handful from ethnic minorities and even fewer people with a disability. The predominant age range is over 45, though there are some in their 20s.

Of the 'younger' ones, i.e. born in 1960 or later, the vast majority have degrees – a third from Oxbridge, 6% from ex-polytechnics and the remainder from universities up and down the country. Most had studied arts or social sciences, but there were also a few from business studies, science and medicine. Of the current Cabinet, six have first and/or second degrees from Oxbridge, seven from Scottish universities, three from ex-polytechnics and a College of Higher Education, the remainder graduated from Hull, Lancaster, Leeds and Sheffield. On the Conservative Front Bench (as at July 2001) Oxbridge predominates.

Member of Parliament is not a first job, so all MPs have experience of working in other areas, from manufacturing to law. However, of those aged 40 or under, almost a quarter had previously worked for MPs or at their party's HQ. A few others had been employed in some of the areas covered in this book such as the media, academia, trade unions, think tanks, lobbying and local government. Also, a third of them had 'cut their teeth' on the election process by previously fighting seats safely held by parties other than their own.

The one thing that all of them have in common (with the exception of Dr Richard Taylor, Independent Member for Wyre Forest) is a history of party activity. Over 40 per cent of the under-40s had been local councillors and just about every MP will have served his or her time as a party activist, helping others to get elected to Parliament or local councils along the way.

Between them, over 600 Members of Parliament are bound to exhibit just about the whole range of human personality traits – some more likeable or laudable than others. In the run up to the 2001 election it was reported in the *Guardian* that the Conservative Party were considering personality questionnaires as part of their candidate selection process. As a dummy run two sitting Tory MPs took the test and came out with profiles that could not have been more different.

Member A was described as – 'Friendly, verbal, influential, persuasive, communicative, kind, persistent, deliberate, dependable, a good listener, accommodating, non-demanding, firm and strong-willed. Can listen to another person's point of view and dislikes confrontational situations.' By contrast, Member B emerged as – 'Competitive, individualistic, demanding, forceful, driving and assertive. Displays confidence in most situations, looks for a quick result and questions the status quo. Is motivated by power, authority and achieving good results. Enjoys challenging assignments, prestige and position and will continually be looking for opportunity and advancement.'

Member B is probably the type of person most people would think of as an MP. Given the adversarial, not to say competitive, point-scoring nature, of the Debating Chamber and, to a large extent, the media interview, Member B might also be predicted to be more successful in the ministerial/frontbench promotion stakes. But there are many ways of being a successful MP; the ministerial route is only one. The traits exhibited by Member A make them eminently suited to the important contributions of MPs to their constituency, the work of parliament and of their party. And if, as many people believe (often regretfully) the focus of power is moving away from Parliament, then the persuasive and co-operative traits of Member A may, in the long run, have more influence on policy. A young Labour parliamentary candidate, Judith Begg (currently working at the Fabian Society), made just this point: 'Working behind the scenes can put pressure on in a way that's more constructive than standing up in Parliament and saying I disagree with this. I think you can put pressure on Ministers if they're in your own party by being less confrontational, saying we like what you're doing, but we want you to go further.' Wherever the focus of power lies now, or will move to in the future, the point is that the Commons is a broader church in terms of personality traits than you might at first assume. And in case you were wondering, and without wishing to foster any gender stereotypes, Member A was female and Member B male.

What every MP does need, however, is self-confidence. This is a difficult trait to define because one person's self-confidence is another's arrogance, but if you are easily crushed or undermined, then becoming an MP would not be a good choice of career. Politicians, and those around them, hold strong views and will argue aggressively to promote them. There are people who intend to reach the top and don't mind who they trample on along the way (though there are also those who can compete effectively without the need to win at another's expense). And, as one former MP's researcher pointed out, some Members do have egos 'the size of Belgium', which can be pretty overwhelming. Plus, as a fair amount of your time will be spent in the public eye, any mistakes or set-backs will be on view, or rather put on view by the media, who are not averse to handing out the odd mauling, so a thickish skin is a definite advantage.

You will also need to have an interest in people, or at least the issues that concern them, as well as the patience to deal with the awkward customers or those who bore you. The ability to show interest and/or liking (or at least feign it) is a requirement for most jobs that involve dealing with the public, but it is particularly important for MPs given that their continued employment depends on alienating as few of their constituents as possible. Likewise, promotion prospects depend largely on keeping in with the right people in the party, or at least not offending the wrong people. This assumes (a) that you have the insight and political nous to identify who the right and wrong people are – who's got the power, or at least is up and coming, and who's on the way out – and (b) that you are both willing and able to be tactful and diplomatic. That is not being cynical. In any organisation, not just Parliament, it helps if you know which way the wind is blowing. It's just that in politics, it is writ large. But knowing who's who and what's what is never enough by itself – conviction, commitment and hard work are all important.

The work

Constitutionally, the role of backbench MPs is to represent their constituency, legislate and hold the government to account. They may also have particular interests, policies or social groups, that they want to defend and promote. Plus, as members of a party they have obligations to that organisation. So their work can be split broadly into four main categories: constituency, parliamentary, party and special causes.

Constituency work. In representing their constituency, MPs work on two levels. They respond to individual constituents' requests for help on all manner of subjects, from asylum appeals to disputes with local councils, health or education authorities etc. This could be during the regular face-to-face constituency 'surgeries' where constituents can turn up to talk to their MP, or via the hundreds of letters received each week. In responding to these queries, the MPs rely heavily on their staff, the work of whom is discussed in the next chapter. If the staff are based in the House (as opposed to the constituency) they in turn will use the Commons' Library facilities and particularly the services of the Library Clerks, as you will see in the chapter on Staff of the Parliaments. Most people will contact their MP only occasionally, but every politician will have their 'regulars' who write to them frequently either to pass on their views in general or to ask for help. Many requests for help are very specific to that individual, e.g. 'my housing benefit has been cut off', 'my local authority won't give planning permission for my extension' or 'my child has been denied the special schooling he needs'. Often the MP is the constituent's last port of call when their own efforts to resolve the situation have failed. The politician then acts as information source, adviser and, possibly, lobbyist on their behalf. For various reasons quite a few enquiries will be inappropriate for the MP to deal with so they will be need to be passed on to other agencies, social services, housing departments etc. But it all takes time. Then, in every MPs postbag there are what Martin Bell and Iain Dale in their interviews call 'the green ink mail' and 'the nutters' respectively. – those who have only a tenuous grasp on reality. Sad though the green inkers may be, they usually can't be helped by their MP.

As well as dealing with queries from individuals, the MP must act as a channel of communication for the various interests within his or her constituency – the industries that provide local employment, health related groups etc. Much of an MP's time in the constituency will be spent on visiting factories, schools, hospitals and so on. While these visits may have the added advantage of keeping the MP's profile high locally, these visits are not just photo opportunities or re-election ploys, they are fundamental to keeping in touch with the local issues and opinions. Without this knowledge, the MP cannot do, and be seen to do, the job properly. Armed with the knowledge thus gained he or she will then feed back into the national debate via the parliamentary work.

Parliamentary work. For many voters, Parliament is about the Punch and Judy show of Prime Minister's Questions, because this is the only aspect of its work which is regularly shown on television. However, most parliamentary work takes place away from the gaze of the broadcast media. The ways of the House are complex and often unwritten. MPs have often said that it takes a long time to fully understand how it works and how to use it to their best advantage. However, some of the methods by which backbench MPs can raise issues of concern to them and/or their constituents and call the Government to account are:

Early Day Motions (EDMs): These are brief expressions of opinion which are printed on the Order Paper (the daily programme of the Commons) and read by all MPs, though they are rarely debated. EDMs are often described as the graffiti wall of the Commons but they do serve the valid purpose of allowing free expression of opinion and gauging Parliamentary support for particular issues. Often they are concerned with parochial issues but they can stimulate debate and sometimes be the starting point of serious campaigns on particular issues. EDMs are now published on the Parliament website if you want to see some examples.

Questions. These can be oral or written. The questioning of Ministers and the Prime Minister is seen as an important weapon in the armoury of MPs in their role as watchdogs of the Executive as well as a way of eliciting the information they require on government action and policy. It should also be said that oral questions in particular are often asked in order to embarrass the Government and score party political points.

Oral questions are taken every day except Friday. Prime Minister's Question Time lasts for half an hour once a week whereas each Minister (and/or their junior Ministers) will answer for about one hour once a month. All oral questions have to be submitted to the House of Commons' Clerks in the Table Office, who will ensure that they comply with the rules of the House. Their advice is not always appreciated by the Members and most MPs will have some tale to tell about how they battled with the Table Office Clerks, and often lost! (For the Clerks side of the story see the chapter on Staff of the Parliaments.) As MPs are not backward in coming forward with their questions, there are always more than can possibly be answered in the time so a number are selected at random, tombola-like, in the aptly but quaintly named 'five o'clock shuffle'. Even so, only a limited number of the oral questions selected will be answered on the day as other Members can ask supplementary or follow up questions which can take up the allotted time. In this case, the outstanding oral questions are given written answers.

Written questions are a more common, and often more effective way, of eliciting specific information from Ministries. Again, MPs use the system to full effect. With as many as 250 written questions a day being tabled, they constitute most of the questions to the House in a year and are an important tool of MPs in their search for answers.

Debates. Many debates take place in a sparsely populated Chamber and though the exchanges seldom alter the opinions of those who hold opposing views, they are still seen as important. Debates are a means of expressing the opinions of MPs and/or their constituents' and of possibly influencing the attitudes of Government Ministers. For example, if the latter see that there is a groundswell of backbench opposition within their own party to a particular measure then it may influence their actions. Plus, local or national press coverage of a debate may help fuel a campaign as well as inform voters on the issues.

Committees. Every Bill must go through the Committee Stage in which it is scrutinised line by line. This takes place in Standing Committees on which every MP will serve at some point. Higher profile in terms of public awareness, are the Select Committees, most of which scrutinise the work of Government Departments and undertake Inquiries on issues within the subject area. Their questioning of witnesses is occasionally shown on TV news and their final Inquiry Reports are sometimes the stuff of press headlines. (The section on the Clerk's

Department in the Staff of the Parliaments chapter will give you more information on Select Committees.) Select Committees allow some MPs (on average there are 11 members on each one) to become more deeply involved in areas of interest to them. This can entail fact-finding expeditions away from Parliament and may include trips overseas. In the Civil Service Fast Stream chapter, Laurie Lee's diary details the visit to South Africa of the International Development Committee from the point of view of the civil servant organising it on the ground.

Party work. The MP relies on his or her local party organisation and supporters, almost all of whom are volunteers, and so it is very much in their interest to work closely with them. Meetings, fund-raising events and so on go on all the time, not just during elections. Plus, as the chief political campaigner in the constituency, the MP can lend important support to candidates in the local elections.

Many MPs will also get involved at national party level. This is not only out of loyalty but also enlightened self-interest. They may be able to influence party policy or strategy as well as possibly enhancing their position with the powers that be. So, there are minutes to be read, agendas to be prepared and speeches to be researched and written.

Work for special interests. All MP will have certain areas that are of particular interest to them (often listed in Parliamentary directories such as Dod's, see Further Information). Depending on what is appropriate for these causes, they may become involved in relevant Select Committees or the introduction of legislation inside the House and/or campaigning outside. Becoming expert on a specific subject and being able to champion the cause can be particularly rewarding.

Some thoughts from a new MP

Paul Farrelly (quoted at the beginning of this chapter) describes his first few weeks as an MP:

Nothing prepares you for the experience of Parliament until you're there as an MP. For the first few weeks I didn't have an office but I did have a pink ribbon on which to hang my sword. The debates in the Chamber are like something out of Monty Python with people bobbing up and down, sometimes for hours on end, hoping to catch the Speaker's eye to make their point. If they succeed it is often entirely unconnected with the debate and more to do with providing a useful quote to their local newspapers. Then you're hanging round pretty much every night until 10 o'clock quite often filling in the time having a drink, talking with people on the terrace or beavering away in the office, before you go and vote. And the question on most people's lips as you go through the voting lobbies is 'what the hell are we voting on this time'. To say the experience is bizarre is an understatement.

But that said, the greatest privileges of Parliament are, first, that you can only be held to account by Parliament for what you say, so you're not restricted by the oppressive libel laws in this country and, second, that if you take a constituent's case to a Ministry, they deal with you promptly. You have a direct line to the top and it works. Previously, as a journalist, I could only have highlighted the case and hoped that someone else would take it up.

As a backbench MP you're not going to change the world but it is important to decide very quickly what you want to achieve and what is achievable, otherwise you could sink into the morass of Parliamentary procedures and flit from one pointless meeting or reception to another without accomplishing anything.

Selection

The final selection procedure is, of course, the general election and all candidates must be nominated on an official form which has to be signed by 10 electors. However, except for Independent members, the process of selecting the individuals who will represent their Party, starts long before that form is completed. Each political party will have its own way of doing things, but it invariably involves a combination of hustings, selection meetings and interviews at both local and national level. These often take place over a period of weeks if not months and can place quite a burden on the prospective candidate if they live and work a long way away from constituency in which they want to stand.

In the 1997 election the Labour Party allowed all women shortlists of prospective candidates, but following a challenge on the basis of sex discrimination, this had to be dropped. However, in the Queen's speech in June 2001, the Labour Government said that it intended to bring in legislation to allow such shortlisting in order to attempt to overcome the imbalance of representation between the genders in the House.

Terms and conditions

The Whips will make certain demands of MPs in Parliament in terms of attending debates and votes, the electorate have the opportunity to dismiss their representative every four or five years and the party can opt to de-select them at intervals, but on a day to day basis MPs are largely in control of the amount of work they do and how they organise it. This autonomy can be a double-edged sword. For those who are happy to do the minimum to get by, it is a definite blessing, but for conscientious MPs there is the constant need to draw boundaries and decide when enough is enough; even in the Parliamentary recesses there is still work to be done, though at a less frenetic pace. So, how many hours they work a day and how much holiday they take, is up to each individual MP. Included in the hours at work, or at least away from home, is the travelling between Westminster and the constituency. Obviously this is not such a problem if your seat is in London or the South East, but for the majority of MPs whose constituencies are many hours away, it can take quite a toll on relationships and family life.

The promotion pathway, in the sense of progressing from back to front bench is very limited. In the Party of Government the starting position is Parliamentary Private Secretary (unpaid assistant) to a Minister, then, if all goes well, up the Ministerial ladder to the Cabinet, or even Prime Minister – though that's about a 1,000 to 1 shot. For those who do not, or do not want to, make it onto the Front Benches, there are various niches they can carve out for themselves as Bruce Grocott mentions in his interview.

The current salary for MPs is £51,822. In addition to this, Ministers receive additional payments according to their seniority. These range from an extra £26,835 for a Junior Minister to £68,157 for Cabinet Ministers and £113,596 for the Prime Minister. MPs who are also MEPs, MSPs or Welsh Assembly Members draw their full Westminster salary but take a reduced salary from the other body (see below).

On top of this MPs can claim various allowances for travel to and from the House on Parliamentary business; towards the cost of maintaining a second home if their constituency is outside London; to cover the costs of office accommodation in the constituency and staff either in the

House or the constituency and, should they leave the House at a General Election, a resettlement grant of between 50% and 100% of their annual salary depending on the age of the MP and the number of years served. You can look up the full list of allowances on the websites of the House of Commons (Factsheets) and/or the Cabinet Office.

Many MPs supplement their income by having professional and business interests outside of Parliament. As long as these activities do not impinge on their ability to carry out the functions of an MP appropriately and they are registered in the required way, this is acceptable practice. (The register of MPs' interests is on the Parliament website.) However, what is, and what is not acceptable, is not always clear cut and many a newspaper headline has cried 'foul' over an MPs external earnings.

MEPs, MSPs and Assembly Members

The split of core work is basically the same as for Westminster MPs, i.e. constituency, party, parliamentary and special interests. However, the types of questions asked and problems posed by constituents might well differ between the parliaments and assemblies and the parliamentary work is certainly different from Westminster. In all the other parliaments and assemblies policy/legislation formulation takes place largely in committees in which all the politicians participate.

The selection procedure is similar to Westminster in that it is by party and then election. Equally all the politicians have a large degree of autonomy about how they organise their time. The stresses and strains of travelling between constituencies and political centres are the same, though for MEPs, of course, it is even worse as the distances are that much greater. Plus there are a number of MSPs and Assembly Members who are also Westminster politicians and so have to shuttle around even more.

MEPs salaries are the same as Westminster MPs. MSPs currently receive £42,493 and Welsh Assembly Members £38,000, though this is reduced by two thirds for those Members who are also MPs and being paid as such. All of them, however, will also benefit from various allowances for travel, subsistence, staff and office costs, etc.

Summary   **Westminster MP**

Role	• To represent their constituency, legislate, scrutinise the Executive and raise matters of public interest
Requirements	*Education*: No particular qualifications required, though majority are graduates
	Nationality: British citizen or citizen of a Commonwealth Country or the Republic of Ireland
	Those ineligible: Convicted criminals serving a sentence of one year or more. Undischarged bankrupts. Serving police officers, civil servants, judges or those in the armed forces.
	Age Limit: None specified
	Equal opps: Open to all
	Relevant work experience: Can be in any sphere
	Postgraduate qualifications: Not required
Selection procedure	• By party and election
Key skills and qualities	• Commitment, confidence, willingness and ability to relate to people from different backgrounds
Pay and conditions	*Salary*: £51,822 (plus extra £26,835 for Junior Minister, £35,356 for Minister of State, £68,157 for Cabinet Minister and £113,596 for Prime Minister
	Expenses: Various allowances for travel, subsistence staff costs etc.
	Hours: At discretion of the MP
	Holidays: At discretion of the MP
	Promotion: To frontbench or Government post
	Job Security: Fixed-term contracts of up to 5 years. In 'safe' seat long-term security is good

Further information

• Paul Flynn, *Commons Knowledge: How To Be A Backbencher* (Seren, 1997).A handbook for new MPs, written in a readable, light-hearted style
• Linda McDougall, *Westminster Women* (Vintage, 1998).

Interviews with many women MPs in the 1997 Parliament. Good insights into Westminster generally and from a woman's perspective in particular

• *Dod's Parliamentary Companion.* (Vacher Dod Publishing Ltd, Annual) MPs and Peers biographies, lists of MSPs, Assembly members, MEPs and lots more. A mine of information.

• *Useful websites:*
House of Commons: www.parliament.uk
Scottish Parliament: www.scottish.parliament.uk
Welsh Assembly: www.wales.gov.uk
N.I. Assembly: www.ni-assembly.gov.uk
European Parliament: www.europarl.eu.int
Cabinet Office: www.cabinet-office.gov.uk

2   Politicians' staff

Politicians' staff are some of the unsung heroes of the parliamentary system. They work long and hard, often in cramped and ill-equipped offices. Some will make working for politicians their lifetime career and others will see it as a shorter-term opportunity to gain experience and knowledge of the political system before moving on to new fields. They may even become politicians themselves or perhaps special advisers themselves, or perhaps Ministerial Special Advisers (covered separately at the end of this chapter).

How many staff a politician employs, where they work, what job titles they use and what they actually do varies. For Westminster MPs the number of staff can range from one to three (full-time equivalents), who may all be at Westminster or split between the constituency and the Commons. MEPs, MSPs and Assembly members will similarly make choices about the number and type of staff they employ. A recent survey of MPs' staff came up with the following categories and job descriptions:

Parliamentary Assistant: Generally a qualified and experienced graduate (or equivalent) capable of conducting, evaluating and interpreting in-depth research on a specialist subject of some complexity. May also assist on more general issues arising from the constituency including casework, and on substantive media contacts.

Executive Secretary/PA: A highly experienced, probably graduate level, assistant. Conducts research in respect of constituency matters or matters of special interest. May progress casework. Substantial external contacts, with e.g. media, lobby groups, constituency parties. Controls MP's diary and arranges all activities. Purely secretarial activities likely to be of secondary importance, at least in terms of time.

Research Assistant or Constituency Assistant: Graduate or experienced person capable of progressing complicated constituency casework; and/or conducting research from several readily available sources, presenting the results in ways which are politically and presentationally useful to the Member. May handle routine correspondence independently and, in constituencies, handle a range of visitors. Drafts and issues press material. In the constituency, a link with the local party.

But obviously these categories have been distilled from the entirety of MPs staff. On the ground, the distinctions are not always so clear. But, whatever the niceties of job descriptions, the workload is certainly varied.

Politicians' staff: some examples

Margaret Payne works for two Labour MPs, Clare Short (Birmingham Ladywood), who is also Secretary of State for International Development and Michael Foster (Worcester). Clare Short has another full-time worker at Westminster and a part-time staff member based in the constituency, whereas Michael Foster has a constituency worker but relies solely on Margaret's part-time help at the Commons.

Because I work for two different people, I have a lot of variety. On a Monday we [Margaret and Clare's full-time Parliamentary Assistant] *will receive Clare's work through the red box. We don't see her much. Her life is spent mainly in the Department for International Development. We do make arrangements to meet at least once a month, usually for lunch or a drink in the evening, but otherwise the only contact is over the phone or via messages. As well as a Cabinet Minister she is a very hands-on, hardworking constituency MP and will often have done an advice bureau in her constituency over the weekend so there could be 25–35 cases for us to plough through. She signs every letter so each day the work we produce gets taken to her for checking, signing and returning to us. Because Clare doesn't have a constituency caseworker we're also constantly dealing with calls from Ladywood plus, of course, the correspondence. Ladywood is quite a deprived area so many of the letters from constituents are about their personal housing, health or immigration problems and we've built up good links with the relevant organisations in Birmingham to help us deal with them.*

On a typical Michael day, and he's here at least three days a week, we will go through the post together and over work I've done or need to do. Michael's constituency is very different from Clare's, more affluent, and the phone calls and correspondence are often about policy and more thought-provoking, for example, recently there has been a lot of interest in the Euthanasia Bill. I keep a database of constituents who contact us about different subjects and make sure that they receive quotes from Hansard when the topic is discussed. That generates more correspondence. This week I've probably written about 100 letters for Michael and, between us, about 80 a day for Clare. Then, of course, there's the filing. Life is a lot more normal now, but when Michael's bill to ban foxhunting was being discussed things just went ballistic. There were days when I would literally spend the whole time opening letters and all the mail had to be thoroughly scanned; we had police protection. I was organising meetings, television and radio presentations. It was phenomenal. The Bill fell in July 1998 but two years on we're still getting phone calls about it.

I do get involved in research for Michael, but I don't write speeches. I give him headings really. I will give him a pack with all the bits I've found in it. He's doing a speech soon to the Guide Association on the influence women can have in the 21st century on politics, so I got him lots of briefings on women's issues in the House and a couple of reports on what it was like to be a woman MP written by two of the 1997 intake.

Now a different Parliament and a different party. Sarah Green and Kathleen Spencer-Chapman work, in London and Brussels respectively, for the Green MEP Jean Lambert. Sarah Green is based in the constituency and works near London Bridge:

I look after Jean's diary in London and the UK because she'll occasionally do events outside London. I also handle all her UK correspondence with constituents, lobbyists, whoever. A lot of that will be on general policy but also on European issues and stuff that's coming up with the European Parliament and the Commission. Jean works on particular issues – anti-racism, refugees and asylum policy – and she's on the Social Affairs Committee so she does a lot on social exclusion and social security issues. Because we're working on that all the time we acquire familiarity with it so I can draft letters on it. It's only sensitive things I would check with Jean. But something we find a lot is that people mix up different levels of government, so people will often write here with problems about housing or something and I just have to explain to them how to get hold of the right person at the right level of government. I don't write speeches for Jean, but I do the background research.

Also I look after quite a lot of Jean's liaison with the Green Party, particularly the people working at the Greater London Authority. Plus, although there's a part-time press officer, I will handle some of this. For example when the BBC are looking for Jean for a comment I'll set it up and maybe talk to them explaining the context of the issue before they get hold of Jean. First of course, I have to track Jean down. Because they work in a number of places we often play the 'chase the MEP' game!

On the other side of the Channel in the Parliament Building in Brussels, Kathleen Spencer Chapman's work is slightly different:

It's a real mixture and changes all the time in response to whatever comes up. There's always the general admin. side, answering emails, filing, correspondence, and so on. I also liaise with people in the Parliament here, such as advisers and press officers, and with Jean's assistant and the Party in the UK. If Jean's going to speak at a conference, I'll do the background research for her speech. All the MEPs are members of committees on particular issues and I follow one of Jean's committees in particular, Justice and Home Affairs. I go to all the meetings and follow what's going on there. I point out to Jean any reports she might want to table amendments to and help draft the amendments. If there are meetings that come up when she's not in Brussels then I'll represent her – sometimes I speak on her behalf if there's something she particularly wants to make a comment on, otherwise I'll just take notes. Keeping up with what's happening in the press is also an important aspect of the job. During the recess I'll be doing some research for a report about social security systems Jean is working on.

So, helping to solve constituents' problems, answering their questions on policy issues, doing background research on all manner of topics, liaising with the media, lobbyists and many others are all part of a week's work. The more mundane things – routine letters, filing, form-filling etc. – have to be done too, and there are downsides. As Margaret says, 'You can work really hard for a constituent and desperately try to

get them what they want, but they're still not happy. They don't understand the system I suppose.' And it can be frustrating to work so hard
with your employer to get something you feel strongly about on the
political agenda only to see it defeated or shelved.

The one thing that staff based in the Parliaments or Assembly don't
usually get heavily involved in is campaigning work at election times,
but those in the constituency will.

Skills, qualities and background

Given the variety of work done by their staff, what should politicians
be looking for when they recruit? Intelligence, common sense,
keyboard and computer skills, tact, stamina, excellent listening and
writing skills (and that includes grammar and spelling), and the ability
to juggle umpteen tasks at once will all come in handy. Depending on
the make-up of his/her existing staff, politicians may specify a particular type of experience, for example liaison with the media or
knowledge of a particular policy area. And I should say that gender is
no bar. Although the three examples here are all female, there are as
many if not more male staff members.

An interest in politics in general is essential and partisanship in terms
of either membership of the party or at the least identification with its
aims is usually required. Margaret Payne is an active member of the
Labour Party and has been for many years and both Kathleen and
Sarah had experiences on their CV that were both practically and
ideologically in tune with their employer's interests. Kathleen had
spent a couple of months in Bosnia on a United Nations High
Commission for Refugees' summer programme as well as a year in
India working with non-governmental organisations (NGOs). Sarah
had likewise done voluntary work via the European Voluntary Service
as well as a spell as a support worker for the charity Mencap and helper
with the Fair Trade Organisation, a small NGO.

There are no specific educational requirements but while the slightly
older cohort of staff may not always have had degrees (Margaret who
first worked in the House in the mid-1980s subsequently got a social
science degree through the Open University) the majority of new
entrants now will be graduates. Sarah has a degree in History and a

masters in International Politics, both from the London School of Economics. Kathleen went to Cambridge and though her final year of study of Social and Political Sciences provides the title of her degree, in fact in her 1st year she studied French and Hindi, in the 2nd year Hindi and Indian Studies and had a 3rd year out in India with NGOs.

A knowledge of another EU language can be useful for MEPs' staff, but it is not essential. Even in Brussels Kathleen knows of people who do get by with just English, though it is obviously better if you can speak French.

Getting in

There is no stipulation that jobs have to be advertised, but some politicians will go this route. The *Guardian* and other quality newspapers, the *New Statesman* and possibly local papers are the main places to watch. Speculative applications may also work, though not if you just mailshot every member. Target those of the political persuasion you are most in tune with, find out about their special areas of interest (listed in books like *Dod's Parliamentary Companion*) and highlight the relevant parts of your education or experience on your CV. The best way still is to use contacts; either ones you already have through university, family or friends or make them by getting involved in the party at local or HQ level. Finally, many people will offer to do voluntary work and hope to use their time in the Parliament or Assembly to get paid work, though this is by no means guaranteed.

Terms and conditions

Politicians have an enormous amount of freedom about the terms, i.e. holidays, hours etc., and how much they pay their staff. Every politician is allowed to claim up to a certain amount for staff salaries, but how they carve up this amount is largely up to them. In practice, research for this book showed that average full-time salaries seemed to be between £18,000 and £24,000 for Parliamentary Assistants/Researchers, though possibly less for some constituency workers. Having said that, on 5th July 2001, Westminster MPs voted to accept the recommendations in the report of the Senior Salaries Review Body (part of which was quoted at the beginning of this chapter) which though it increases the staff salaries allowance to a maximum of £60,000 per year (£70,000 for London constituencies) also puts limits on the flexibility of pay rates. Recommendation 4 of the report says that 'New staff should be employed on agreed pay scales which would apply to all MPs' staff'. (p.9) These scales, with rates for London and elsewhere respectively, are: Parliamentary Assistant £28,500 & £24,000; Executive Secretary/PA £27,000 & £22,000; Research Assistant or Constituency Assistant £23,500 & £18,500; and, for more purely secretarial roles, Executive Secretary £22,500 & £17,500; Senior Secretary £20,000 & £17,500; Junior Secretary £17,000 & £12,500.

Moving on

For those staff who decide to move on, the experience and knowledge they have gained will often help them to get into other careers related to their political interests. Lobbying companies look favourably on ex-researchers and assistants and will advertise vacancies in the *House Magazine* (the in-house journal of Parliament). Working at Party HQs or for non-governmental organisations, going into journalism, moving into the civil service and more are all possible next steps.

Summary   **Politicians' staff**

Role

- To assist the politician with the various aspects of their work including constituency casework, correspondence, background research of policy issues, possibly speech writing, liaison with the media.

Requirements

Education: Degree in any discipline usually a requirement for new entrants

Nationality: None specified

Age limit: None specified

Equal opps: Open to all

Relevant work experience: May be specified

Relevant postgraduate qualifications: Not usually required

Selection Procedure	• Advertisements may appear in national press, journals such as *New Statesman* and possibly local press. Personal contact and speculative applications. • Application usually by CV and selection by interview
Key Skills and Qualities	• Communication, organisational, keyboard and computer skills; commitment, tact
Pay and Conditions	*Salary*: Negotiable. Salaries of current staff average £18,000–£24,000 *Promotion*: No promotion pathway *Job Security*: Contracts are usually for the duration of the Parliament *Political activity*: Allowed

Special Advisers

In employment terms, the 70 plus Special Advisers are hybrid creatures straddling Government, Civil Service and Party. They are appointed by Ministers, employed by the Civil Service and have close links to the Party.

The nearest thing there is to a job description is the Model Contract for Special Advisers (1997) which says, 'Special Advisers are appointed to advise the Minister in the development of Government policy and its effective presentation.' and that their duties could include:

✓ 'reviewing papers as they go to the Ministers, drawing attention to problems and difficulties, especially ones having party political implications, and ensuring sensitive political points are handled properly;

✓ 'devilling' for the Minister [researching], and checking facts and research findings;

✓ preparing speculative policy papers which can generate long-term policy thinking with the Department;

✓ contributing to policy planning within the Department,

contributing ideas which extend the existing range of options available to the Minister;

✓ liaising with the Party, including the Party's own research department, to ensure that the Department's own policy reviews and analysis take full advantage of ideas from the Party; and encouraging presentational activities by the Party which contribute to the Government's and Department's objectives;

✓ helping to brief Party MPs and officials on issues of Government policy;

✓ liaison with outside interest groups to assist the Minister's own access to their contribution;

✓ speech writing and related research, including adding party political content to material prepared by permanent civil servants;

✓ providing expert advice as a specialist in a particular field.'

In other words, not only can Special Advisers be involved in developing policies, they also work to ensure that the Party and the Government are in synch over matters of policy and help to orchestrate its presentation via the media. Most Ministers will have two advisers. One will probably be more concerned with policy formulation and the other with presentation, though of course the two roles overlap considerably. Colloquially known as 'policy wonks' and 'spin doctors' respectively, the former will often have a background in the Departmental specialism, for example Foreign Affairs, Education, Health etc. and may come from any of a number of the areas covered in this book, including academia, think tanks and trade unions. Spin doctors will usually come from journalism or press office backgrounds. Of course the largest concentration of Special Advisers are in No. 10 working directly with the Prime Minister.

Forward Planning. Obviously Special Adviser is something to aspire to, a few years down the line when you have gained the right sort of experience. But, just in case you're wondering…Selection is at the discretion of individual Ministers. Salaries are organised in three pay bands ranging from £27,503 to £80,453 as at 1 April 2000. The general employment terms of Special Advisers are quite complex, but there is full information in the *House of Commons Library Research paper 00/42, 5 April 2000* available on the House of Commons website.

Further Information

* *Dod's Parliamentary Companion,*
* House of Commons website www.parliament.uk.

Interview: **Bruce Grocott**

Bruce Grocott has worked in academia and television and was a Labour Member of Parliament for almost 20 years.

CV

Education	BA Politics, Leicester University
	MA (Econ), Manchester University
Career	1963–4: Administrative Officer, London County Council
	1964–5: Politics Tutor, Manchester University (part-time)
	1965–72: Lecturer & Senior Lecturer, Birmingham Polytechnic
	1972–4: Principal Lecturer, North Staffordshire Polytechnic
	1974-9: MP for Lichefield and Tamworth
	1979–87: Producer, Central Television
	1987–97: MP for Wrekin
	1997–2001: MP for Telford

Do you come from a political family?

Dad's a Labour voter, though not active in the Party, but I come from a Labour family. When I was about 18, just before I started my degree, I started going along to local Labour Party meetings and then I was active at university in the Labour Club.

I can't remember a time when I wasn't interested in politics, domestic and international. I went to university specifically to do a politics degree. I was offered places at the more fashionable universities of the time like the London School of Economics and University College, London, but they didn't do politics degrees, so I went to Leicester.

Was it the ideology, or the practical application of politics which interested you?

All of it. I was interested in the personalities, in elections, in political theory, in systems overseas, you name it and I was interested in it, and have remained so all my life.

After your degree, you carried on to a Masters?

Yes, but not straight away. I got places to do my Masters when I finished my degree but I couldn't get the money, so I spent a year working as an administrative officer at the London County Council (LCC), which, of course, no longer exists. After that I went back to study at Manchester University and used the knowledge gained from the year at LCC to write my thesis on local government. I also did some teaching at the University while I was studying.

So was it a conscious decision to go into academia?

Well again it was pursuing my political interests. It just seemed the natural way of carrying on doing the things that I enjoyed.

Did you enjoy lecturing?

Yes I did. I taught a mixture of undergraduates and people on day-release courses while working in local government and in social work, which I liked. When you're teaching you get a lot back from the students whatever age they are and whatever their background, but I must admit I did particularly enjoy the ones that were on some of the professional courses like social work for example. Some of them were pretty keen on politics and were politically active.

At the same time as being a lecturer, when I was about 30, I was also a local councillor on the Council where I lived which was in Bromsgrove

I suppose I always preferred the sharp end. Even when I wasn't a councillor I was active in the Labour Party. I've always enjoyed the practical side of it more than theorising about it, although I do enjoy the theorising as well.

When did you decide you wanted to be an MP?

I don't know really. I was just more and more active – vice chairman of the local Labour Party and a councillor. I didn't just wake up one morning and think 'I want to be an MP'. It's not a sudden leap, it's usually a result of years of active party politics. I was fascinated by politics so the idea of the life of a politician would always have seemed attractive to me, but it's a long jump from that to thinking that you're actually going to be one. I wouldn't say I thought about that seriously until my late 20s.

When did you first stand for Parliament?

That was in 1970 [aged 30]. It was South West Herts, a safe Tory seat and near to my original home town of Watford.

Isn't it demoralising fighting a seat you know you can't win?

No, it's very enjoyable in the sense that you haven't got great responsibilities. No one's expecting you to win the seat. One of the many advantages of having an academic background in politics is that I knew a lot about it and have never believed, as I think many MPs and candidates tend to, that they could buck trends. I know pretty well how the electorate moves in Britain and basically if the tides in, it's in, for one party or another. I never expected to win the seat but that didn't alter the enthusiasm with which I involved myself in the contest.

Then you won Lichfield and Tamworth in 1974.

The second time, yes. There were two elections that year, in February and October. It was pretty obvious as soon as the February one was over that it wouldn't be long before the second one because there was no overall majority. It was almost a permanent election that year. I didn't lose by that many in the February and was quickly re-selected as the candidate. I was mightily pleased when I won in October.

Can you remember your feelings when you won?

Relief. I'd hoped to win in the Feburary and thought I stood a good chance and was very disappointed. You're not just disappointed for yourself but also for the many volunteers that are with you when you fight an election. Politics is an entirely voluntary activity in this country. You are dependent on active members of your party. Obviously I'd been an active member of the party a long time myself so I'd helped a lot of other people, but it is very disappointing when you lose.

But then you lost in 1979.

Well that was less disappointing because I really did see it coming. I didn't expect to win. I was prepared for it. There was a very small majority, one of the most marginal seats in the country. I was almost anxious to get on with life. I had young children and I could see this bulldozer coming at me but couldn't do a great deal about it until it was over. Then I just got on with the next phase in my life; you have to.

When you lost, did you still have in your mind that you wanted to get back into the House at some point?

I wasn't really thinking about that, to be honest. I'd got two young children and my wife had given up her job as a social worker to be my secretary/agent so we were both out of work at the same time. You don't have much time to comtemplate your navel when you're in that situation.

So how did you get the job at Central Television?

Just luck I suppose. Well it's not uncommon for ex-politicians to work in the media — Edwina Currie's doing it now, I think. Obviously you've got some experience of it because you're in the media a fair bit when you're a politician; you know how it operates. I worked initially as a presenter, reporter and researcher on Central's political programme, which suited me and them. Then I worked my way through and ended up producing Central Weekend, which is still running, I'm happy to say.

What were the satisfactions of doing that type of work?

Oh it's just terrific fun. Television is the most fun of the various jobs that I've been in, though politics is the most important. It is just very enjoyable and there's a product. That's what I liked about it. Three of us launched Central Weekend *in 1986 and it really was a one-off; to have an hour and a half live on a Friday night was unique in those days. It was a huge programme with a big studio audience, and guests and good budgets. The beauty of it is that each week you've got a product. You start on Tuesday, we used to have Monday off, and work till midnight on a Friday night when you put the programme out. If it was a good one great, if it wasn't then you'd got to do better next week. The other jobs that I've been in, politics and lecturing, are much more hamster in a wheel type jobs, there isn't quite a beginning, a middle and an end, its continuous.*

But in 1987 you came back to the House and have been there ever since. What keeps you there?

First and foremost knowing that it really is a very, very important job. I'm not being pretentious about how well any individual might or might not do it, but I do believe very strongly in democracy and that if it is to work then the people who fulfil the representative function have to be hard-working, decent, honourable etc. I think if that ceases to be the case then it is very bad news. It is a very important job to do well and I have never lost that sense of it. And the mixture of work is very satisfying. What you do locally in the constituency keeps your feet on the ground but you can also make a contribution to politics at a national level. You have to accept that there isn't just a lever to pull and everything happens exactly as you want it; it never will in a democracy, that's part of the nature of the system, but you can still get things done.

It's certainly a very varied job and there are many, many different ways of being a good MP. Some will devote themselves almost entirely to a particular specialism, an important area of work. One who did that spectacularly was Jack Ashley in Stoke. Although he did all the other work as well, he made a particular specialism of the concerns of people with all kinds of disabilities. Or you can concentrate on the

Ministerial structure which means that you spend proportionately more time at Westminster than in the constituency. Yet another way is to be, in effect, a nearly full-time constituency MP. They're all different and all valid and all satisfying. Some people enjoy enormously communication via the media, some much prefer via public meetings and conferences, the skills of addressing a conference are very different from doing a three or four minute interview on television. People find what they're good at and what they enjoy doing. But having said that, the relentless demands of the job, mean that a fair chunk of all MPs work is in common. You cannot, well you don't want to, avoid the facts of the job which are huge numbers of letters arriving from constituents every day, surgeries in the constituency and demands from groups and schools and factories and churches and everything else in your constituency. There's a basic routine of the job which would occupy at least half of anyone's life I would think whatever kind of MP you are, but the how you spend the other 50% of your time is up to you to define.

What sort of person would not make a good MP?

Someone who didn't like people the company of other people – listening to them, talking to them, trying to solve their problems – that's number one. If you ever get to the stage where you don't like going to the school, the factory, the public meeting or the pub, then you're going to find life a bit difficult as an MP.

You've certainly got to have a coherent set of principles which is a rather pompous way of saying that you have to have some passion for the values of the party that you're representing. Apart from anything else you get hundreds of issues to deal with and if you're not looking at it from a framework of beliefs you will simply be starting at square one with every query – you would have to stop and think where am I on this one. In very simple terms I'm a socialist, a lifelong member of the Labour Party, and I do believe in, to coin a phrase, 'for the many not the few'. By and large if you are faced with requests from people who don't have much power themselves for whatever reason then you're much more instinctively sympathetic and supportive to them than you are to those with plenty of power of their own. If you've got a hundred letters on your desk and some of them are glossy brochures from successful organisations saying will you back us on this or that, and another one is a poorly written letter from a widow who's not getting her benefit, you shouldn't need to think for very long about which of those two cases you deal with first.

I suppose you need to be reasonably confident of who you are and where you're coming from. You get knocks in all walks of life, but they are very public in politics. And, finally, you mustn't be overawed by the environment at Westminster; you wouldn't be very good at your job if you were. You're not here in order to be here, you're here in order to do a job for the people who elected you and for the party that you've given your life to representing.

3   The staff of the parliaments

The Palace of Westminster employs around 1,000 staff in all manner of posts from caretakers to Clerk of the Commons, with hundreds of people in between: IT specialists, administrators, researchers, security staff and many others. It is almost a self-contained world with numerous cafes, bars and restaurants as well as a gym, a hairdresser and other facilities. The turnover of staff is relatively low. Even where there are the inevitable workaday gripes about pay and conditions, people still seem to have enormous affection for the place, and even long-serving employees retain a sense of the importance and excitement of working at the centre of national politics.

It is obviously impossible to look at all the opportunities available in Parliament (many of which will require minimum qualifications of GCSEs or A levels), so this chapter will concentrate on staff in the three departments which are most likely to be attractive to graduates with an interest in politics – the *Official Report* (*Hansard*), the Library and the Clerks Department. There will also be information on similar posts in the Scottish Parliament. However, for the reason given in the introduction, I have not approached the Northern Ireland Assembly. Also, no detailed information was available from the Welsh Assembly, though I understand that many of their posts are filled via the Civil Service with vacancies being advertised in the regional press.

Working in the Parliaments, whether it be at the *Official Report*, in the Library or the Clerks Department or their Scottish equivalents, brings its own rewards and challenges. However, you must remember that all these roles exist to facilitate the work of the politicians. If your aim is to do something on your account – to make things happen – then think carefully about your choice. Indirectly, of course, you will be contributing greatly because you will be aiding the Members (and at Westminster, the Lords) to carry out their business. But, you will not be directly influencing affairs and there is a strict limit on the amount of party political activity you can undertake even in your own time.

The Commons Official Report

The *Official Report* of debates in the Chamber and in Standing Committees, known as *Hansard*, is made up of many individual pieces of work which are put together like a sort of verbal patchwork.

Each *Hansard* writer takes a five- or ten-minute section of ragged speech and meticulously turns it into polished prose. Under the watchful eyes of the Sub-editors, these short pieces are joined together to become a coherent whole. All of this is done at speed so that the finished product can be published as soon as possible. In the case of the debates in the Chamber, this is by the next morning or sometimes a little later if the MPs kept talking after 1.30 am.

A lot of people assume that Hansard is very much a verbatim report and I think they're quite shocked when they find it isn't. Jude Wheway, Committee Reporter

They'd be even more shocked if it was an actual verbatim report! Emma Brazier, House Reporter

Erskine May, the bible of Parliamentary procedure, defines the *Official Report* as one which '. . .though not strictly verbatim, is substantially the verbatim report, with repetitions and redundancies omitted and with obvious mistakes corrected, but which on the other hand leaves out nothing that adds to the meaning of the speech or illustrates the argument.'

As Emma Brazier says, reporting MPs' speech in this way is '. . . a linguistic challenge. How do you turn a jumble of words into coherent sentences, get to the kernel of what the person's trying to say and keep the flavour of that person's speech – you wouldn't report Dennis Skinner in the same way as the Prime Minister.'

The following example shows the craft involved in the work. The first version is the verbatim record of the contribution of a current

Member of Parliament to a Standing Committee debate. The second is Jude Wheway's 'translation' which is about 16% shorter than the original and a good deal clearer:

Verbatim: *Just briefly, Mr O'Hara. These touch on obviously issues that are clearly nobody argues about what's important in terms of rights, entitlements and procedures. I will without formally opposing or forcing a division on the amendments reserve our position on them. I think my friend and I will want to go and take some further careful advice. We wanted to have the debate now. I don't pretend to be an expert, having been spared serving on the Committee of the Immigration and Asylum Bill and having not been transferred to this particular brief by that stage until the very end. I am an expert on the last amendments that came in on Report stage. I am aware of those but not much of the other detail, but I am aware also of the general provisions. We will look at this. We may want to come back to it. I am grateful for the indication that clearly both procedures are clearly remaining to be capable of judicial review. That must be right.*

I have just had one other reflection and it is this, which is that there may be a case, it seems to me, and we need to look at it probably even more so – I will refer to it again in a second, if I may, in the context of the human rights legislation – for more clearly creating a division of the High Court that deals with administrative and/or immigration and asylum matters, and just as the court has developed, as it were, divisions or areas of expertise in the commercial courts and in the family court and so on, it seems to me that, although clearly you don't have simply an administrative law area because that can apply across the whole range of public policy and lawmaking. None the less, in areas of expertise, and although there may be a de facto nomination of the individual judges to deal with these sort of matters, because a) the law has changed, changes a lot anyway and because other considerations apply, the interrelationship, there may be an issue, it's not a Home Office matter principally but it may have Home Office input, for suggesting to the Lord Chancellor and to colleagues in other Departments that we look at the way in which we organise things. We need not just to have, to use the phrase from elsewhere, fair and as fast as possible decisions, but we need to have decisions that are clearly made by competent and experienced authorities whether they are adjudicated by tribunals or judges, and we need to make sure that they are fully qualified to do that. I just observe that we are moving into an area where it may be wise to think through the judicial structures as well as the tribunal and administrative ones.

Jude's Version: *No one would argue that the issues touched on here are important in terms of rights, entitlements and procedures. I will, without formally opposing or forcing a division on the amendments, reserve our position on them. My Hon. Friend the Member for West Aberdeenshire and Kincardine and I will take further advice on the matter. I do not pretend to be an expert, having been spared serving on the Standing Committee for the Immigration and Asylum Bill. I was not transferred to this brief until the end of its deliberations, so I am an expert only on the final amendments that were tabled to it on Report. I am also aware of the general provisions of that Bill. We shall examine this matter further and may wish to come back to it later. I am grateful for the indication that both procedures will remain capable of judicial review; that must be right.*

I have a further reflection on the matter, which may need to be examined in greater detail, and to which I shall refer again later in the context of human rights legislation. It is that there may be a case for creating more clearly a division of the High Court that deals with administrative and/or immigration and asylum matters. The courts have developed areas of expertise, for example in commercial courts and family courts. One does not have a specialised area of administrative law, as that applies across the whole range of public policy and lawmaking. None the less, although there may be a de facto nomination of individual judges to deal with matters such as these, the law has changed a great deal and other considerations and interrelationships apply. There could, therefore, be a case for suggesting to the Lord Chancellor and colleagues in other Departments that we should re-examine the way in which we organise these matters. That may not principally be a matter for the Home Office, although it could have Home Office input.

We need – to borrow a term used elsewhere – fair decisions to be made as fast as possible by competent and experienced authorities, whether they are cases before tribunals or judges. We must ensure that those people are fully qualified to make those decisions. It may be wise to think through the judicial structures as well as those of the tribunals and the administration.

(Apart from one or two very minor changes by the Sub-editor, this is how it finally appeared.)

Some speakers are more fluent than others, but it would be a brilliant MP indeed who always finished a sentence and never made a grammatical error. The *Hansard* writers make good the verbal deficiencies. In his book *Commons Knowledge: How to be a Backbencher,* Paul Flynn MP pays tribute: 'The *Hansard* writers buttress their great skills with uncanny intuition. Never once has a Member made a grammatical mistake. Even hopeless gibberish appears as cogent argument. Missed words and even lines in quotations miraculously appear. All MPs owe the *Hansard* staff a debt of gratitude.'

So who are the *Hansard* writers and how do they work?

Committee Reporters: The main role of Committee Reporters (previously called Transcribers) is to report the proceedings of the Standing Committees, i.e. those Committees that scrutinise bills clause by clause. Tapes are made of each Committee meeting, and using these plus written notes of who spoke when, the Committee Reporters produce the official record.

Though the Committee Reporters work from tapes, do not be misled into thinking they are just audio typists. As you saw from the example above, there is a great deal more to it. In order to edit the speech so that it reads fluently Committee Reporters need to '. . . get a handle on what the MPs are talking about. They debate so many different subjects and just researching five minutes' worth of debate you can be checking facts on the internet or with colleagues in the House, finding out who people are and so on. Every day is a school day here.'(Jude Wheway).

Each Committee Reporter works on usually five- or sometimes ten-minute sections of tape; this is called a 'turn'. For their first turn of the day they may be able to go into the committee room itself and make their own notes as well. Thereafter they will work in the Committee Reporters' Room on tapes plus written 'logs' of speakers which are provided by the Committee Sub-editors who sit in throughout the Committee's meeting.

Of the 27 Committee Reporters employed overall, teams of 7 will work on each Committee's debates. Depending on the complexity of the speech or subject matter of the turn, the transcription can take anything up to an hour. Because the Committee Reporters' turns are not consecutive, they will not necessarily be able to follow the line of the argument and may need to liaise with team members working on other parts of the debate. The Committee Sub-editors on the other hand have the advantage of hearing everything: 'The problem the Committee Reporters face is that they have five minutes of words; it might not start with a sentence, and sometimes it doesn't have a sentence all the way through. They're coming cold to a subject and they don't know how a Member started his speech...the Committee Sub-editor has the benefit of having been in there and understanding what the member was saying and the context.' (Lorraine Sutherland, Deputy Editor.) So, after the Committee Reporters have done their work, the Sub-editors will ensure that all the parts are accurate and fit snugly together. Ideally, the finished product will be published the next day or at least in time for the next Committee meeting.

House Reporters: House Reporters record the proceedings in the Chamber of the Commons. Like the Committee Reporters, they also take five- or ten-minute turns, and most work from tapes, though there are a minority who use shorthand. Unlike the Committee Reporters, however, the House Reporters always attend the debate when it is their turn and from their bench on the front row of the Press Gallery in the Chamber, they make their own logs (and take their verbatim notes if they use shorthand). In fact, there are always two Reporters present, the one whose turn it is and another to act as an extra pair of eyes on the lookout for sedentary interventions which as Emma explains are ' . . . Members shouting out. The interventions only go into the *Report* if the person making the speech picks up on it'. 'Or if they're very funny – though we shouldn't really', adds Lorraine Sutherland with a smile. When the Chamber is quiet, two House Reporters may seem unnecessary, but when it's crowded, for example during Prime Minister's questions, they will both have their work cut out keeping track of things.

At the end of their turns the House Reporters go back to their shared room and, like the Committee Reporters, will work on their parts of the patchwork before passing it on to the House Sub-editors for final checking.

Requirements: Committee Reporter is the entry point for Hansard writers. After three to five years, and providing there are vacancies, promotion is to House Reporter. Thereafter, but again only when vacancies occur, it is on to Sub-Editor of whom there are 16 for the Committees and 8 for the House. The Editorship and three Deputy posts complete the promotion pathway.

Although a degree is not actually required for Committee Reporter, in practice most of the applicants for the 8-10 training places a year are graduates from a variety of disciplines. Some have recently graduated but many are older with (often unrelated) work experience which is the way Paul Hadlow, the Training Manager, likes it: 'We do take people straight from university but I wouldn't like to pack a training programme with people like that. I also want people with a bit of experience of the nasty outside world'. Jude Wheway whose work was quoted above had spent twenty years as a theatre stage manager. In 1998 she completed an Open University degree in Politics, left the theatre and joined *Hansard*. On the other hand, Emma Brazier, who after 6 years as a Committee Reporter is now a House Reporter, came straight from her degree in Politics at York. (The two people quoted may be female, but there are also a number of male Reporters and in recent intakes the gender split has been roughly 50/50.)

Applicants need good keyboard skills, though the 3-4 month training on the techniques of *Hansard* and the ways of Parliament will include typing courses, if necessary, to get trainees up to the 65wpm required. An interest in politics, good general knowledge, the ability to 'turn a sentence', and an eye for detail are also required. The selection procedure involves an application form with a piece of verbatim speech to be corrected and edited, a general knowledge test, a tape transcription and a panel interview.

Given the hours to be worked, it would probably be better if you were not the sort of 'morning person' who is good for nothing after 4 in the afternoon. Transcribers work 14.30 to 22.30 on Mondays; 10.15 to 24.15 Tuesdays and Thursdays; 10.15 to 18.15 Wednesdays, although it is 9.30 to 15.30 Fridays. House Reporters definitely need to be night owls as they work until whatever time the House rises which could be in the wee small hours.

It's not altogether flippant to add that House Reporters need a reasonably good head for heights. The Press Gallery in which they sit is very steeply banked and as the House Reporters sit on the front bench, they look straight down onto the floor of the chamber. Perhaps because of this, it's apparently quite usual for new House Reporters to have the same recurring dreams – either that they drop their pads and pencils onto the politicians below or that they themselves fall into the chamber.

Pressure is an integral part of the work. There is a limited amount of time available for each turn and the whole thing has to be completed to a very strict deadline. Hansard writers must be able to work consistently under this pressure and to the deadlines imposed on them by the tight publishing schedule.

Benefits: The holiday entitlement is 28 days rising to 40 days plus Bank Holidays. And, when the House is in recess, shorter hours are worked at the management's discretion.

Starting pay is acknowledged to be on the low side for London at £15,112 but after the training period is over Committee Reporters do receive an extra £4,000 or so night allowance in recognition of their late working hours. Free taxis are provided home (within a 20-mile radius) after 10.30pm. The Committee Reporters' pay scale goes up to £26,189 and the House Reporters' scale is £24,521 to £31,658 plus night fees.

But for those who work at *Hansard*, it is obvious that the major benefit is being a part of, and party to, the political process. 'It's a great job for anybody who's interested in current affairs, especially in the politics of this country. You are right in the heart of it and it does feel like that. When you're sitting in the Chamber at Prime Minister's Question Time it's really exciting.' (Emma Brazier)

The Lords' *Official Report* (Hansard)

The Department of the *Official Report*, House of Lords, is completely separate from that of the Commons and has its own Editor and hierarchy. It is a smaller operation because the House of Lords has far fewer committees off the Floor of the House, but its remit is exactly the same as for its Commons counterpart, i.e. to produce an edited verbatim report of the proceedings by the following day.

All the 15 writers are called Reporters, although two of them are more senior and are designated Chief Reporters. The latter are responsible for reporting the proceedings of the Grand Committees, which are the equivalent of Standing Committees. Unlike the House of Commons, all but three of the Lords Reporters use shorthand (pen or machine), and a shorthand speed of 160wpm is normally an entrance requirement. In fact, the majority of Reporters (approximately one third or whom are male) are from a court or conference reporting background and most have had previous experience with the *Official Report* on a freelance basis. A degree (or equivalent) in any discipline is required.

Select Committee reporting in the Commons and Lords

You will probably have noticed that no mention has yet been made of reporting Select Committees. This is because the *Official Reports* are not responsible for recording the proceedings of these Committees in either the Commons or the Lords. In fact, the responsibility lies with the Department of the Clerk of the House in the Commons and the Parliament Office in the Lords. In practice, however, it is dealt with in both Houses by an independent firm or company. This is currently W.B. Gurney and Sons, the senior partner of which holds the formal appointment of Shorthand Writer to the House in the Commons and Official Shorthand Writer in the Lords.

The actual work of reporting the evidence sessions of the Select Committees (33 in the Commons and up to 12 in the Lords) is done by 11 permanent Reporters and between three and eight freelance Reporters according to the workload, plus 3 freelance Tape Loggers/Transcribers. Reporters (using shorthand) may do turns in a meeting of anything from 10 to 60 minutes or even an entire session of three hours or more. The Tape Loggers/Transcribers will be present throughout a meeting to make a log and note useful terms and names, but then produce the transcript from the tape.

Because of the nature of evidence sessions of Select Committees, the reporting is required to be much more verbatim than the *Official Report* and thus less editing is required, although grammatical errors still need to be corrected and false starts and redundancies erased. There are no

Sub-editors and each Reporter or Tape Logger/Transcriber is responsible for producing the finished transcript within a time frame of up to 4 days.

There are occasional Trainee Reporters vacancies open to those with 130/140wpm shorthand and 50 wpm typing. Or, for those with faster speeds and relevant experience, it is possible to go straight in as a Reporter. A degree is not required though a good general knowledge is essential. The average age of entry for Trainee Reporters and Reporters is 24 and 28 respectively.

Summary	**The Commons' *Official Report* (Hansard), Committee Reporter**
Role	• To provide an edited verbatim report of Standing Committee debates by transcription of direct tape recordings. (House Reporters: To report speeches and proceedings in the Chamber of the House of Commons)
Requirements	*Education*: No minimum educational requirement stated, but most applicants are graduates from a variety of disciplines.
	• Good keyboard skills.
	Nationality: None specified
	Age Limit: None
	Equal opportunities: In general, Parliament encourages applications from all. However, the *Hansard* section of the building (including the Press Gallery) cannot accommodate wheelchair users. Working from tapes, hearing impairment is also problematic
	Relevant Work Experience: None specified, will take on new graduates, but do like to receive applications from those with work and life experience.
	Relevant Postgraduate Qualification: None
Selection procedure	• One or two intakes per year of usually 5 people. Approximately 250 applicants for the 5 places
	• Vacancies advertised in the *Guardian*, *Evening Standard* and on the Capita RAS website (see Further Information)

- Application form from Capita RAS with written test to correct short verbatim speech

- General knowledge test (consisting of 98 questions) and a tape transcription test plus an interview by a panel of three people

Key skills and qualities

- Good grammar and general knowledge, ability to understand a complex argument, to work under strict time pressures and as part of a team.

Pay and conditions

Starting salary: £13,112–£26,189 plus approx. £4,000 night allowance at end of (3–4 month) period of training. Taxi home, within approx. 20 mile radius, after 10.30pm.

Hours: Monday 2.30pm to 10.30pm; Tuesday and Thursday 10.15am to 12.15am; Wednesday 10.15am to 6.15pm; Friday 9.30am to 3.30pm.

Holidays: 28 days rising to 40 days plus Bank holidays. Leave must be taken during recesses at Christmas, Easter and Summer. Shorter hours, at the management's discretion, are worked during the recess.

- 9-month probationary period

Job security: Very good

Promotion: To House Reporter (of whom there are 16) after 3–5 years. Salary scale is £24,521 – £31,658 plus night fees which average around £4,500 per year. Reporters work until the rise of the House, whatever time that is. Promotion from Reporter is to Sub-editor of whom there are 16 for Committees (scale £31,710 – £47,972) and 8 for the House (scale £35,914 – 58,164)

- Staff must not engage in party political activities.

Summary   Lords *Official Report*

Role

- To produce an edited verbatim record of the proceedings of the House of Lords.

Requirements

Education: A degree (or equivalent) in any discipline,

- Shorthand 160wpm (pen or machine)

- Typing 65wpm

Nationality: None specified

Age limit: None

Relevant work experience: Most successful applicants have court/conference reporting experience and have worked in the Lords as freelancers

Selection procedure

• Recruit as and when necessary, but usually one or two people a year. There is an application form and interview, but most candidates are known to selectors through freelance work.

Key skills and qualities

• Sound knowledge of English language, excellent general knowledge, ability to work under pressure and as part of a team.

Pay and conditions

Starting salary scale: £24,975-31,096 plus a night duty allowance of £1,270.

Hours: Monday – Wednesday from 2.30pm and Thursday from 3.00pm until the rise of the House, usually around 10.30 – 11.30pm. Not many Friday sittings, but when there are hours are 11.00am to 4.00 or 5.00pm.

Holidays: Six weeks per annum plus statutory holidays.

Job Security: Very good

Promotion: To Chief Reporter/Assistant Editor (equivalent to Commons Sub-editor) of whom there are 6. Salary scale £31,283–£47,399 plus £2,048 night allowance. Thereafter to Deputy Editor and Editor.

Summary

House of Commons and House of Lords, Select Committee Trainee Reporters

Role

• To provide record of proceedings of Select Committees

Requirements

Education: Good general education: degree not required.

• Shorthand (pen or machine) 130/140wpm.

• Typing 50wpm (direct entry as Reporters requires higher speeds.)

Relevant Work Experience: Not required for Trainee Reporter (but essential for direct entry as Reporter)

Selection procedure

- All recruitment and selection carried out by W.B. Gurney and Sons, 7 Millbank, London SW1. Tel: 020 7233 1935

- Trainees are employed as and when necessary, one at a time

- Posts are advertised in the *Evening Standard* and *The Times*

Key skills and qualities

- Good grammar and general knowledge, grasp of an argument, ability to learn technical terms, and work under pressure.

Pay and conditions

Salary: Trainees start at £18,000. Promotion to Reporter at starting salary of £23,000 and going up to £30,000

- Three-month probationary period in both cases.

Hours: To fit in with Select Committee timings. Averages out at 35 per week, with usual finish around 6.pm on Tuesdays, Wednesdays and possibly Thursdays

Holidays: 28 days plus bank holidays for Trainee Reporters; 33 days rising to 38 days plus Bank holidays for Reporter

Summary

Scottish Parliament *Official Report,* Trainee Reporters

Role

- To provide edited verbatim report of proceedings in the Chamber and Committees of the Scottish Parliament

Requirements

Education: A degree in any discipline

- Good command of English

- Knowledge of Scottish Politics

- Typing skills not required, training will be given

Nationality: none specified, but 3 years UK residency required

Age Limit: none

Equal opportunities: Open to all. Building is wheel-chair friendly

Selection Procedure

• There are 24 Reporters. Recruitment takes place as and when vacancies occur

• Vacancies advertised in the *Scotsman* and *Glasgow Herald*

• Application form with a piece of verbatim speech to edit. Then a general knowledge test, tape transcription and editing test. If successful at this, then on to interview

Key Skills and Qualities

• Good grammar and general knowledge, ability to understand complex arguments, to work under pressure and as part of a team.

Pay and Conditions

Salary: trainees scale £14,000 – 20,647

Promotion promotion to Reporter after 6 months training, scale £17,822 – 24,282. Thereafter promotion to Sub Editor on £23,153 – 32,961

Hours: Reporters are expected to be available (bandwidths) 8.30am to 7.30pm, but in practice are unlikely to work so long. Mondays, Tuesdays and Fridays tend to be 9.30am to 5.30pm with Wednesday and Thursday (parliamentary days) possibly requiring attendance to 7.30pm

Holidays: Five weeks plus statutory holidays

Information and Research Staff

The House of Commons Library Department: The Members' Library in the Commons is just as you would imagine it – traditional and imposing, with a gallery, book-lined walls and an air of exclusivity. Sad to say, however, only a handful of the 200 or so Library staff work there. Most of them are based in a very ordinary office block a few minutes walk away from the House at No. 1 Derby Gate. This may not be so beautiful, but it is far more appropriate for the wide scope of work undertaken by the Library.

The efficient storage and dissemination of information (enormous amounts of it, both physical and electronic) is crucial to the smooth functioning of the House. The Commons produces hundreds of documents which have to be organised and catalogued – the MPs questions and other business have to be indexed, and books, journals, pamphlets and official documents stream in from outside. The cataloguing and indexing of this vast array of material falls to Library staff who hold librarianship or information science qualifications. For example, Beatrice Jamnezhad works in the POLIS unit (Parliamentary Online Indexing Service) and, amongst other things, she is responsible for indexing Parliamentary Questions. This involves condensing down 40 or 50 word oral questions to a maximum of 13 words before entering them onto the database. She also works on material from the Lords as well as keeping a watching brief over entries to another part of the database. However, the public contact that Beatrice had enjoyed in her previous job as a librarian in a public library, is maintained through weekly stints at the House of Commons Information Office which answers questions from the public on anything and everything to do with Parliament.

Whilst many of the qualified library staff have an interest in politics which will have influenced their decision to work in Parliament, their initial career choice would have been based on an attraction to information work in whatever setting. If this is true of you, you can find out more about careers in librarianship from the Library Association (contact details in the Further Information section). To most graduates with a desire to work in or around politics, however, it is the role of Library Clerk which would probably be more immediately attractive.

Library Clerks (also called Researchers): Organisationally, the Library is split into a number of sections and sub-sections and the 37 full-time equivalent Library Clerks work in all but two of them. However, by far the majority (29–30, plus 7 Heads of Section who are also Library Clerks) work in Research Services where their role is to provide information and briefings for MPs and their staff.

This is done both by responding to specific requests from particular Members (or their staff), and by the production of a number of Research Papers each year. Often these papers are concerned with subjects on which the House is legislating or give regular statistical information, but they can also be more general for background briefings. For example, amongst the 99 papers produced in the year

2000, there were titles such as 'Russia: The Presidential Election and Future Prospect's; 'Advisers to Ministers'; 'Cannabis'; 'The Tourism Industry'; 'Shifting Control? Aspects of the executive-parliamentary relationship'; and 'Common European Security and Defence Policy: A Progress Report'.

Because of this variety and the complexity of the information to be provided, the Research Service is split into seven sections each dealing with specific subject areas, i.e. Business and Transport; Science and Environment; Social Policy; Social and General Statistics; Economic Policy and Statistics; International Affairs and Defence; Home Affairs. The last deals with the topics of Parliament, the constitution, local government, civil and criminal law, police, religion, arts, media, immigration, gambling and licensing. As well as the Head of the Home Affairs Section, there are 3 other Library Clerks, one of whom is Arabella Thorp, an Edinburgh Law graduate who then went on to study music. She was happy to describe her CV as 'odd', though in fact that combination of subjects is quite a good mix given the nature of the Home Affairs section.

In any one year, Arabella will write three or four Research Papers, either on her own or with other Library Clerks. For example, her 51-page report in April 2000 on the Section 28 Debate of the Local Government Bill (prevention of the promotion of homosexuality) was written in collaboration with a colleague from the Social Policy section. Research Papers are substantial reports which need to be well-researched and accurate, but there is also considerable time pressure, as Arabella describes. 'A Research Paper may have to be written in as little as a week, though we might be able to do some background work on it beforehand, and we do have to consult outside interest groups to find out what their views are.' Because the Research Papers are briefings for all MPs, not just those with a specialist knowledge of the subject, they have to be written in a way that is intelligible to all. The salient points must be clearly laid out so that the MPs, who have many other calls on their time, can absorb the information quickly. All Research Papers are now published in full on the House of Commons website, so you can see for yourself how detailed but also how readable they are.

The number of Research Papers written by each section will vary, but in all the divisions, the Library Clerks spend the bulk of their time responding to requests for information from the Members. These requests differ in purpose and urgency. Policy information for a speech at a specified time in the future, allows the Library Clerk to plan their workload in advance. However, a call from an MP who's appearing on Newsnight in an hour demands an immediate response. Some of the questions asked of Library Clerks will relate to policy issues, but many of them are in response to issues raised at MPs' surgeries or in their postbags and are therefore very specific to the constituent's problem. The volume of this type of nittty gritty work will vary between departments. The Social Policy section which covers health, social security, education, housing, and personal social services will probably get more than most, whereas those concerned mainly with statistics will get least. In Arabella's case in Home Affairs, the split is around 50/50 policy to constituency questions.

Periodically each research section records a weekly 'snapshot' of the more substantial queries they receive. In one week in February 2001, Arabella's Head of Section, Edward Wood, recorded the following enquiries (deadlines shown in brackets):

✓ How can someone change their name by deed poll?
✓ Divorce – complications as a result of one party being subject to power of attorney
✓ What are the opening hours for a parish poll?
✓ General briefing on the Divorce (Religious Marriages) Bill
✓ Government policy on domestic violence
✓ Bureaucracy and paperwork affecting the police (same day)
✓ Independent members on the new local government standards committees (two days)
✓ How can a British citizen born abroad get a copy of their birth certificate? (two days)
✓ Local government referendums (three days)

Most of these enquiries were from backbench MPs helping constituents with problems, but one came from a senior opposition spokeswoman in connection with her frontbench duties.

Some of these questions would require straightforward, factual answers amounting to just a page or two, but others would obviously involve a good deal of research and a fairly substantial written response.

And, these are just the main recorded queries. Each day Library Clerks will probably have to respond to a number of quick telephone queries, so although they try to complete all work without specific deadlines within two weeks, this is not always possible. The ability to prioritise and work under pressure are therefore crucial. As Arabella Thorp says this level of autonomy is a 'very important and distinctive aspect of the job. You're solely responsible for all the enquiries in your particular subject area and for managing your own time and workload. But also, your anwers go straight to the Member who needs the information. This is very different from even high-level jobs in the civil service and makes a big difference to my enjoyment of the job.'

Selection and promotion: The minimum qualification is a first degree, but in practice many of the successful applicants have a postgraduate qualification and possibly related work experience. Posts are advertised in the *Guardian*, graduate publications and relevant professional journals and application is by form and an assessment centre. The latter may vary slightly from section to section but will usually include a written and group exercise to check out candidates analytical, research and communication skills.

Promotion is to Senior Clerk after 4 years, subject to satisfactory performance, and with it comes a substantial pay rise. Thereafter it is to Head of Section, but as there are so few of these posts there can be a long wait. This can be frustrating for staff who want to take on new challenges, but there are some other opportunities in the meantime. In the next section on Clerks, you will read about Committee Specialists and it is possible for Library Clerks to take secondments to these posts. The Scottish Parliament and Welsh Assembly can also offer opportunities for secondments. Should you want a complete change, there is the possibility of an unpaid career break of up to 5 years.

The Lords: There are currently 5 Library Clerks in the Lords and vacancies occur only occasionally. The work is slightly different in that there are no subject specialists and no research papers. Most of the Library Clerks' time is spent responding to Members queries which can be on any subject. The terms and conditions are broadly similar to those in the Commons Library. The starting salary scale is the same, although promotion to Senior Library Clerks brings a pay band of £32,065 –

£48,584. Hours are normally 10 to 6pm though you may be required to undertake evening duty once a week at an additional £1,861 p.a.

The Scottish Parliament, Research and Information Services: There are 41 staff, including the Head, Janet Seaton (who previously worked in the Commons Library) with approximately a 50/50 split between information and research staff. Unlike the Commons Library however, information staff do not necessarily need to have a library qualification although they do need to have had experience in some kind of information provision.

Because the Scottish Parliament organises its business much more around Committee work, the nature of the work of the Research Specialists (equivalent to Library Clerks) is different to Westminster. The first call on research staff time is to the Committees they work with. Requests from individual Members have to take a lower priority, although of course, the staff will try to meet all the deadlines set. Research Specialists work closely with the Convenor and Clerks of the Committees when they set their programme of work for the session and they can be involved in advising on possible witnesses and special advisers as well as the subjects for inquiries. They also write a large number of briefing papers, though they are not as long as the Commons' Research Papers.

Graham Ross (first degree Sociology, MSc Criminology and Criminal Justice, both from Edinburgh) joined in September and works with two Justice Committees. He attends many of their meetings, which in the case of one committe is weekly and the other fortnightly, and has provided questions for the witnesses as well as producing a number of 4–6 page briefing papers. To write short papers on complex subjects is not easy. A recent briefing by Graham was on the subject of female offenders and gave summaries of reports and research findings on: the background to offending; the causes of offending behaviour, for example drug and alcohol addictions, abuse, mental ill health etc.; the appropriateness of imprisonment; patterns of offending; prostitution; and the latest developments. It was just six pages long.

There are 19 Research Specialists, one of whom is solely concerned with commissioning research from outside organisations. Because the

Scottish Parliament is so new, there is no history on which to predict how many vacancies will come up each year, though it will obviously be in single figures. When openings do occur, they are advertised in the *Scotsman*, the *Glasgow Herald* and possibly the *Guardian*. All contracts are permanent, except where they are to cover a secondment. Applicants must have a 2.1 degree in, or relevant to, one of the devolved subject areas, i.e. agriculture, economic development, education, environment, health, law and order, local government, social work, transport. They must also have some work experience in the area (in Graham's case it was three years part-time voluntary work with the charity Victim Support) and a postgraduate qualification is encouraged. The starting salary is £17,722 – £24,282.

Summary   House of Commons, Library Clerks

Role	• '...to respond, orally or in writing, to requests from individual Members and to prepare briefing papers on subjects of public and parliamentary concern.' (*Graduate Appointments in Parliament 1999–2000*)
Entry requirements	*Education*: Minimum 2.1 honours degree.
	Nationality: British
	Age limit: None
	Equal Opportunities: Applications welcome from all
	Relevant work experience: An advantage
	Relevant postgraduate qualification: An advantage
Selection procedure	• Posts are advertised in the *Guardian* and, where appropriate, specialist press, e.g. *New Scientist* for Science and Environment section
	• Application form and assessment centre. Latter will vary slightly, but usually consist of group discussion, role play (given pack of information to brief MP) and a written exercise
Key skills and qualities	• Literate, accurate, tactful, impartial
Pay and conditions	• Most posts are permanent, but temporary contracts do come up to cover for staff on secondments and career break.

Starting salary scale: £20,000 to £27,500.

• Non-contributory pension

Hours: 10.00am – 6.00m Monday to Thursday and
9.30am-4.30pm Friday when House sitting, 9-5
during recess. Plus one night per week for 2 years
(£2,115 pa)

Holidays: 28 days rising by two days per year for first
two years, then by one day a year thereafter to a
maximum of 40.

Probationary period: Two years

Promotion: Routinely after 4 years (subject to satisfactory performance) to Senior Library Clerk £35,710
– £47,072. When vacancies occur to Head of
Section £35,914 – £58,164. Thereafter to
Directorate

• Cannot be involved in party political activity

Summary   **Scottish Parliament, Research Specialist**

Role
• To provide information to Committees and
individual MSPs

Entry requirements
Education: Minimum 2.1 degree in, or relevant to, a
devolved area, i.e. agriculture, economic development, education, environment, health, law and order,
local government, social work, transport

Nationality: None specified

Age limit: None, retirement age 60

Equal opportunities: Applications welcome from all

Relevant work experience: Some required, amount not
specified

Relevant postgraduate qualification: An advantage

Selection procedure
• Posts are advertised in the *Scotsman, Glasgow Herald*
and sometimes the *Guardian*

• Application form. Interview usually involving a
presentation or a practical exercise, e.g. advising
Committee X using given information

Key skills and qualities
• Knowledge of area; ability to work under pressure;
excellent communication skills, analytical ability

Pay and conditions

Salary scale: £18,722–£24,820 (there are 9 Research Specialist posts)

Hours: Flexible working to make up to 37 hours per week between 8am and 7pm when averaged out throughout the year

Holidays: 25 days rising to 30 after 10 years plus 10 public and privilege days

Probation: 1 year

Promotion: By application and selection board to Senior Research Specialist, 8 posts on scale £23,153–£32,961, then to Principal Research Specialist, 2 posts on scale £33,060–£43,699.

• Limit on the degree of political activity

Clerks

Clerks in the House of Commons: 'The Clerk's Department is responsible for providing advice and services to the House as a whole, the Speaker and Deputy Speakers, the Committees appointed by the House and their Chairmen and Members' (*Annual Report of the Department of the Clerk of the House 1999/00*). In other words, the Clerk's Department is responsible for facilitating the daily work of all the Members and ensuring that their legislation, debates and reports conform to the rules and customs of the House. To do this, the Department is split into 8 sections: the Table, Journal and Vote offices, the Legislation Service, the Committee Office, the Parliamentary Office of Science and Technology and the Office of the Supervisor of Parliamentary Broadcasting.

The Table Office compiles the daily agenda of business. This has the official title of Order of Business, but is often known as the Order Paper. It also produces Future Business, which deals with questions to be asked, motions to be tabled, and Early Day Motions. The latter are MPs' expressions of opinion, which are put in writing but very rarely debated. However, the main part of the Table Office's work is advising Members on how to frame questions and motions so that they comply with the rules of the House.

Clerks in the Journal Office compile the Votes and Proceedings (known as 'the Vote') which are the official minutes of the House.

Somewhat confusingly for outsiders, the Vote Office has nothing to do with producing 'the Vote' but does issue the official publications needed for the conduct of business and manages the printing and publishing requirements of the House. It also operates the Parliamentary Bookshop on Bridge Street, which is open to the public.

The Legislation Service was previously known as the Public and Private Bill Offices. Amongst other things, it provides Clerks for the Standing Committees and ensures drafts of Government and Private Members' Bills conform to the rules of the House. The Committee Office, as its name suggests, is the organisational home of Select Committee Clerks whose main role is the organisation of inquiries and subsequent report drafting. Because of the sheer number of Select Committees the Committee Office is by far the largest section in the Department.

The Overseas Office 'maintains contact with Commonwealth and foreign parliaments at official level and provides information and instruction on the rules and practices of the United Kingdom Parliament. It provides the secretary to the United Kingdom delegations to the Parliamentary Assembly of the Council of Europe, the Western European Union and the North Atlantic Assembly.' (House of Commons Factsheet). The Parliamentary Office of Science and Technology (POST) analyses issues of interest in the two areas in its title and serves both the Commons and Lords, as does the Office of the Supervisor of Parliamentary Broadcasting. What follows is a look at some of the work in the Committee and Table Offices.

Working on a Select Committee: Of the 270 or so people employed in the Department, about 70 are Clerks. Of these, 16 are women and one of them is Lynn Gardner, Clerk of the Agriculture Committee. She became a Clerk in 1991, but had worked previously for the Department in a rather different capacity. After a degree in English from York and a year teaching in Italy, she just needed a job to earn some money and saw a basic clerical post advertised in the Clerk's Department. Though her own day-to-day work was pretty mundane, the environment of the Commons got Lynn interested in politics. She took a part-time masters degree in Politics and Administration at Birkbeck College, London, and decided to apply for a Clerkship.

Her first 'posting' was on the Trade and Industry Select Committee which at that time was carrying out an inquiry into the Iraqi Supergun Affair. For those too young to remember, this concerned the export of manufactured components from a British company to Iraq with whom our relations were anything but cordial. Ostensibly these items were for industrial purposes but turned out to be for military use. Criminal proceedings followed and questions asked of politicians about who knew what when 'This was probably quite unlike any other inquiry I've ever done', Lynn says, 'It was more like a detective story, trying to work out the end. There was a lot of public and press interest, so it all seemed exciting, terribly intense. But at the same time, we were also doing a more standard inquiry into trade with China. It was quite difficult going from one to the other but I think that's an important part of the work here. You do some things that are routine but which in many ways are more important than the exciting things.'

Clerks just starting their careers are obviously given the support they need, but they are also expected to learn fast, as Lynn remembers. 'I had responsibility quite early on for doing an inquiry of my own into trade with China which means finding out about the areas you should be looking at in the first place, drawing up the terms of reference, identifying sources of evidence, writing to people and getting them to submit evidence, and organising programmes of witnesses. We went on a visit to China and I was responsible for organising that in consultation with the embassies in the various places we were going to.'

Obviously, it's the MPs on the Select Committees who decide which areas they want to look into, but then it's down to the Clerks to map out the territory. Recently the Agriculture Committee decided to look into organic farming and having talked around the issue generally, it was left to Lynn to draft the terms of reference for the Committee to approve: 'I thought about the areas they'd mentioned and how they linked to other things and to work other people have done, so there's not too much repetition. In fact, the Lords had done a report last year and we keep files of press cuttings and releases from the Ministry of Agriculture of Fisheries and Food, so we're up to date with what's happening. From all that, I drafted a list of headings for the Members to consider including in the inquiry.'

Having worked with the Agriculture Committee for a while now,

Lynn has become very knowledgeable about the subject area, but Clerks do move to new Committees and need to adapt. Jacqy Sharpe is one of the Principal Clerks of Select Committees, and understands this very well: 'The ability to change subject quickly is fundamental to the work. My great challenge was a committee inquiry into rugby and the only thing I knew about it at the beginning was that the ball was oval shaped rather than round. It was a real learning experience.'

Lynn Gardner feels that the constant need to learn is one of the major rewards of the work: 'It's very satisfying getting to grips with a subject that you may not know much about at the beginning, but is important to a lot of other people. It's actually about real life; being able to put other people's questions to Ministers and get responses then writing a report that can make a difference. It has an intellectual satisfaction in that in the report you're pulling together information from a variety of sources and producing a document which will explain often very complicated issues in a way that other people can understand.'

The average length of time for an inquiry with 3 or 4 evidence sessions would be 6–8 weeks preparation, then the evidence gathering, and just a month or so thereafter for the Clerk to draft the report and get it agreed and published. The extent to which Members and Specialist Advisers (outsiders appointed on a fee basis) get involved in the drafting of a report varies, but because of her experience on the Agriculture Committee, Lynn is mainly responsible for the first draft: 'Obviously Members can amend it as much as they like, but they don't tend to make too many changes. I've only had to re-draft one report because the amendments were so significant.' However, having done all that work the Clerk's name does not appear anywhere on the finished product. Anyone who wants to be publicly acknowledged for their work should not join the Clerk's Department. As Lynn says, 'you are behind the scenes. It doesn't mean you can't have a personality, or that people don't appreciate your work, but you do have to be able to stand back.'

Those people with very strong political viewpoints may also find the work too limiting and frustrating because ultimately the subjects and scope of inquiries is decided by the MPs. This doesn't mean that Clerks don't have strong views, some do but 'you have to be able to be completely bi-partisan', says Lynn. 'It's different from the Civil Service where they have to act for each party of government as they come along. We really do have to be able to deal with any individual from any party and give them the best advice and also write things from their point of view if necessary. You just have to learn that something is out of your hands once it's given to the Committee.'

The Table Office: It may seem a strange title, but the Table Office is so called because until quite recently (the 1940s in fact, which is quite recent in parliamentary history) all its business was carried out at the Table directly in front of the Speaker in the House of Commons Chamber. Now, it has its own rooms, but is still located very close to the Chamber. The name also gives no indication of one of its main functions, i.e. advising MPs on form and procedures.

'The Table Office is a one stop shop for procedural advice.' This succinct description is delivered dryly by Matthew Hamlyn, Deputy Principal Clerk and member of the Clerk's Department since 1987 when he left Oxford with a degree and postgraduate studies in English. 'Essentially we deal with the process of handling parliamentary questions from MPs to Ministers. That is by far the bulk of our work. We take about 40,000 questions a year. We also deal with the processing of around 1,000 Early Day Motions (EDMs) which are essentially expressions of opinion by MPs and get printed on the House's Notice Paper and can be used to continue or initiate campaigns on various subjects. But we also provide general procedural advice on almost anything.'

The information sought by MPs can range from the routine, such as 'how can I table an amendment to a particular bill', to the more urgent – 'how can I stop a debate that's taking place'? Sometimes, the requests can be downright flippant, as when Matthew was asked for the name of Don Quixote's horse for a crossword. But whilst the questions may often be straightforward, the answers may not, as Matthew explains. 'The House of Commons is a self-regulating institution and it agrees its Standing Orders or rules, like the rules of cricket or tennis or whatever. But also quite a lot is not written down. Rather like the distinction between Statute, Case and Common Law, there are the written rules but also a whole series of decisions taken by successive Speakers which form the basis for other interpretations.

'We're a bit like company secretaries. The go-getting business men and women who want to do things and make their millions need to be reminded of what the Companies Act says and when you have to file your accounts and things like that. It doesn't mean the company secretary is going to stop them doing anything exciting, but you do need to ensure that what they're doing is on a sound footing in terms of the law of the land. We have reasonable discretion; the rules aren't applied in a purely mechanistic way. There must be some sort of structure, but we don't want to cause pointless grief and stop Members pursuing legitimate causes.'

But if they're thwarted, do MPs always appreciate that the regulations have to be enforced? 'When you explain the rules to Members, they often want to know why. They want to know the origin of the rule and why it stops them doing what they want to do. Sometimes this can involve lengthy discussions and arguments, which on their side may occasionally become heated. There are a few Members who are convinced we're in a conspiracy with whomever it might be they don't like. Others just regard us as nit-picking bureaucrats, but we are there to enforce the rules the House has agreed to. You have to be not only expert but as plausible as possible at putting your advice across.'

So being able to argue persuasively and enjoy the cut and thrust of debate are two necessary qualities for a Clerk in the Table Office to which Matthew would add in his deadpan delivery, 'the ability to get on with people however they're behaving'. But as with all jobs there are aspects which seem more mundane. 'There is a huge amount of what high-flying graduates might think of as crushingly dull. Words are very important in this place. They have to be right, so there is a lot of checking and double-checking and making sure the right pieces of paper are put in the right place at the right time. Some of it is very routine so you do need detail people, though we're not all anoraks. Detail, logic, persuasiveness and plausibility – it's quite an interesting mixture.' And it's not just applicable to the Table Office; other procedural officies, e.g. the Legislation Service, require a similar mix of skills.

Committee Specialists: All Clerks are permanent employees of the House, but there are also some staff in the Committee office who are employed on temporary contracts (initially 2 years with possible extension for 2 more). These Committee Specialists are employed by specific Select Committees for their particular expertise and they must have at least two year's relevant work experience. Apart from the occasional secondment of Library Clerks, this usually means that the Specialists have had experience of working environments outside the Commons, or indeed the public sector generally, and so they can bring a new perspective.

One such 'incomer' on the Environment, Transport and Regional Affairs Select Committee is Katie Smith. Having been brought up in Scotland, she graduated in Geography from Edinburgh in 1991, and went on to do the professional qualification in town planning at Strathclyde University. She worked for a few years in private economic and planning consultancies in Scotland and Liverpool, and gained experience in dealing with the public sector, mainly advising local authorities and central government on urban regeneration. However Katie wanted to move to London and, in her own words, 'got sick of being in the private sector and having to get up at 5 o'clock in the morning', so when she saw the job advertised in the *Guardian* she applied.

Eventually she was called for a one-hour interview which may not sound much, but was, she says '...very daunting. I was faced with two MPs one of whom was the Chairman of the Committee, a Principal Clerk, The Clerk of the Committee and a Personnel Officer. The moment my bottom hit the seat they bombarded me with policy-related questions. I think if you're not used to what is quite a politicised dialogue you would have been completely fazed. But I got the job and started in January 1998.'

Although taken on because of their specialist knowledge, in practice the Specialists often do very similar work to the Clerks. Lynn Gardner had said this was true on the Agriculture Committee and Katie confirms it: 'on my committee there are three Clerks for the Committe and its two Sub-committees. I share an office with the Environment Sub-committee Clerk and we basically divide up the work by giving whoever's available full charge of any inquiry. In that sense, I do exactly the same job as a Clerk. What I don't do is actually sit next to the Chairman in the meetings as I don't have the procedural knowledge. The Clerks have much more of an overview and understand the Order

Paper and things like that. But it's quite mutually beneficial in as much as I'll ask them about procedural matters and they'll come to me for policy matters.'

Committees use their specialists in different ways, but what has struck Katie is the difference in workplace culture between Parliament and the private sector. 'When I first arrived I wanted to stand up in front of the Committee and say these are the sort of issues I know about, if you want any advice come to me. But that sort of private sector, in your face, approach is not encouraged. I like my colleagues very much, but I would say that the atmosphere in the Department can be quite adversarial; less facilitating or encouraging than I was used to. There are a lot more women coming up now and people from difference educational backgrounds, but even so, I think it might take time to change.'

Coming from the private sector where people expect to get the credit for the good work they do, as well as the brickbats for their mistakes, Katie finds life in the Clerk's Department can be both frustrating and comforting. 'You'll probably write 10 to 20 reports in 4 years and some can be quite large, the size of a PhD thesis, but your name won't be mentioned. Possibly worse, your beautifully drafted questions may get completely mangled or not asked at all. But the upside is, well, yesterday for example, they had a debate in Westminster Hall on one of the reports I drafted and it was really exciting. Members were standing up and arguing cogently because they knew they would get lots of exposure and so had prepared well. Also, I got thanked by my Chairman and that's in Hansard. It's a job where maybe you don't get the highs like you do in consultancy work, but also you don't get the big lows. The Chairman at the end of the day takes the decision and takes the flak – that's quite a nice position to be in.

Clerks – selection and promotion: The entry grade is Assistant Clerk, of which there are 9. Promotion after 4 years is to Senior Clerk (19 posts) and thereafter, when there are vacancies, to Deputy Principal (27) and Principal Clerk (9). Above this, there are three more posts with no generic grade title and then the single Clerk of the House, i.e. the Head of the Department. These titles are pay and seniority grades, but do not necessarily coincide with job titles. For example, someone at the Assistant Grade level working with a Select Committee would be called a Second Clerk but would become the Clerk of the Committee when they reached a higher grade and had more experience. A Clerk will move within and between sections throughout most of their career, so their job titles may change even if their pay grade remains the same.

The minimum qualification for Assistant Clerk is a degree in any discipline and selection for the two or three Assistant Clerk vacancies each year is through the Civil Service Fast Stream (plus a Department Final Selection Board for all applicants who pass the civil service selection board and have put Clerk as their first choice). Please see the chapter on the Civil Service for more information on the application and selection procedure. However, there is also another possible way to become a Clerk.

Whenever there are more than the usual two or three annual vacancies for new Clerks, the Department will accept applications to the Senior Clerk grade from appropriately qualified and experienced staff (such as Higher Executive Officers or Senior Executive Officers) working anywhere in the House. So, it is possible for graduates to start as, say, a Sales Assistant in the Parliamentary Bookshop, a Secretary or an Executive Officer (and the majority in all these kind of jobs are graduates) and work their way through over a number of years. As you currently have to spend at least one year in each grade before applying for promotion, this is not, of course, the quickest of routes, but it is possible.

Terms and conditions: Throughout their careers, Clerks will move from section to section and, in the case of the Committee Office, from one Committee to another. Although the time spent in each place will vary, some sections have a specific 'tariff' – for example, it's four years at a time in the Table Office. The time spent on each Committee will depend on a number of factors, but would not usually exceed 6 years for a senior post and usually two or three years for a more junior one.

For those at Deputy Principal Clerk (DPC) level there is also the opportunity of a two- or three-year secondment to the the Civil Service in the Foreign and Commonwealth Office and the Cabinet Office. Senior Clerks and DPCs may also spend 2 or 3 years on secondment in the recently created National Parliament office in Brussels.

The normal working hours are 10.00am to 6.00pm Monday to Thursday and 9.30am – 4.30pm on Fridays, although of course longer hours have to be worked at busier times. In addition, most Clerks in the procedural offices, and a number in the Committee Office, will do one or two nights a week (when the House is sitting). There is additional payment for this. Holidays are a minimum of 28 days (to be taken when the House is in recess) and the starting salary is around £20,000. Assuming satisfactory performance, this will rise to £31,710 after 4 years on promotion to Senior Clerk..

The House of Lords: As with the other departments, the Lords is a seperate entity. David Beamish is the Clerk of Committees and Clerk of the Overseas Office in the Lords and describes the organisation in the Upper House and how it differs from the Commons.

'We're much smaller with about 20 career Clerks. Although we've got 10 or 11 Clerks in the Committee Office, 4 of those are temporary, normally civil servants who've taken early retirement or come to us at 60 because our retirement age is 65. That reduces the dominance of committee jobs for career Clerks, though every new Clerk will sooner rather than later be in the Committee Office.

'The work on Select Committees is essentially the same. On the whole the terms of reference are not something we get very excited about in the Lords. You give the Committee fairly general terms of reference and trust them to be sensible. As in the Commons, Specialist Advisers are outside experts selected for particular inquiries and they may help the Clerk in drafting the final report. We have just one Specialist Assistant (equivalent of Committee Specialist in the Commons) and that's on the Science and Technology Committee.

'However, we do have two legal staff (qualified lawyers) who work mainly with the European Committee. As there are no Standing Committees in the Lords we have just two Clerks in the Public Bill Office and because the volume of questions is much smaller than in the Commons we don't have a Table Office; everybody just takes a turn on the rota to receive questions, and it's the same for night duties.

'We do have a Judicial Office with two Clerks managing the progress of cases through the highest Court of Appeal; that obviously has no counterpart in the Commons. Unlike the Commons we use a Clerk as Establishment Officer in charge of personnel matters and we have a permanent arrangement with the Cabinet Office to lend them one Clerk as Private Secretary to the Leader of the House and the Government Chief Whip on a two to three year secondment.'

The application and selection procedures and the pay scales are the same as for the Commons, though the title of the entry grade is Clerk, not Assistant Clerk as in the Commons. Promotion is normally to Senior Clerk after four years, but thereafter it depends on vacancies being available. And do the Lords look for a different sort of person? David Beamish thinks not. 'The qualities we look for are essentially the same though I think I'd say that my colleagues in the Commons might require a thicker shell than we might need. Although most of the members in both houses are easy to deal with, there are perhaps more awkward customers in the Commons, if only because there are more ambitious people on the way up. You might say most Lords Members have passed the peak of their career. On the whole, I think Clerks who are successful in one house are likely to be successful in the other, though moving between the two has never really been an option. After a while you get to know both the Members and the practices of the particular house and you'd have an awful lot of re-learning to do.

If I were asked for the two most important qualities for a Clerk, one would be excellent drafting skills and the other would be the ability to get on effectively with Members of all types. The cantankerous genius may have a place in the Civil Service, but I don't think they'd last long in Parliament.'

Summary   **House of Commons, Assistant Clerks**

Role	• Clerks are responsible for providing advice and services to the House as a whole, the Speaker and Deputy Speakers, the Committees and their Chairmen and to individual members of the House.
Entry requirements	*Education*: Minimum 2.2 honours degree or equivalent in any discipline
	Nationality: None specified

Age limit: None (in practice in recent years oldest recruit was 31)

Relevant work experience: None specified

Relevant postgraduate qualification: None specified

Selection procedure

• As for the Civil Service Fast Stream (please see Civil Service chapter)

• Following success at CSSB, applicants who have put Clerk's Department as first choice will attend a departmental Final Selection Board in June or July prior to taking up appointment in October.

Key skills and qualities

• Analytical, drafting and communication; discretion, ability to work under pressure

Pay and conditions

Salary: starting salary is usually £20,000 but could be slightly higher according to qualifications and relevant experience

• Non-contributory pension

Hours: 10.00am –6.00pm Monday to Thursday and 9.30am-4.30pm Friday + possible night duty (for which additional payment is given)

Holidays: Minimum 28 days per year to be taken when the House is not sitting

Promotion: Routinely after 4 years (subject to satisfactory performance) to Senior Clerk (£31,710–£47,972) and thereafter, depending on vacancies and performance, to Deputy Principal Clerk (27 posts), Principal Clerk (9 posts), 3 untitled senior posts and Clerk of the House. Possible opportunity for asecondment to a Civil Service department, currently in Foreign and Commonwealth Office and Cabinet Office. (Existing members of staff in the Commons on an appropriate grade can apply for Senior Clerk positions if there are more than two Clerkship vacancies in any one year.)

Job Security:Very good

• Cannot be involved in party political activity.

(NB: Clerk – Lords -The details are almost identical to above, however the starting grade title is Clerk (not Assistant Clerk) and promotion after Senior Clerk is to specific job titles, e.g. Clerk to the Select Committees.)

Summary **House of Commons, Committee Specialist**

Role
- 'Principal duties will include giving assistance to the Clerks of the Committee in preparing briefing material, drafting reports and conducting analysis for the Committee in support of its inquiries.' (quoted from job advertisement)

Entry requirements
Education: Minimum second class honours degree or equivalent professional qualification plus a minimum of 2 years relevant practical experience (some Committees may specify more)

Nationality: None specified

Age limit: None

Relevant Work experience: Required

Relevant Postgraduate Qualification: Useful

Selection procedure
- Posts are advertised in the *Guardian*, in professional journals relevant to specialism being sought and on Capita RAS website and often in Committee press notices which are posted on the Committee's website

- Application form

- Committees have leeway and many will ask for a written piece of work

- Then usually a panel interview

Key skills and qualities
- As for Clerk

Pay and conditions
Job security: Posts are fixed term; initially for two years and with possibility of extension for a further two.

Salary scale: £19,995–£31,658 according to qualifications and experience.

- Non-contributory pension

Hours and holidays: as for Clerks

Summary **Scottish Parliament, Assistant Clerks**

Role
- As in the House of Commons and Lords the role of the Clerks is to facilitate the work of the Parliament. There are a total of approximately 65

Clerks who work in teams consisting of a Clerk Team Leader, Senior Assistant Clerk and Assistant Clerk. Recruitment takes place into any level, however the entry point for new graduates would be Assistant Clerk

Requirements

Education: Degree in any discipline (though English or Politics may be particularly favoured

Nationality: None specified but must have leave to work and a minimum of 3 years continuous residence in the UK

Age limit: None (retirement age is 60)

Equal Opportunities: Applications welcome from all

Relevant work experience: Experience of working with committees is desirable

Relevant Postgraduate Qualification: None

Selection procedure

• Application form requiring description of relevant skills and experience. Written test of presentation plus panel interview

Key skills and qualities

• Oral and written communications; interpersonal; analytical, IT; adaptability

Pay and conditions

Starting salary scale: £17,912–£22,023. All increases from starting point are performance related based on appraisals

Hours: Flexible with 37 per week, though probably more when Parliament is sitting

Holidays: 25 days up to 30 after 14 years, plus 10.5 public and privilege days

Probation: One year

Promotion: to Senior Assistant Clerk (£23,153–£32,961) then to Clerk Team Leader (£31,000 – £43,699). Promotion is on merit as and when vacancies occur

Political activity: No national political activities are allowed, but permission can be sought for local involvement further information

Further Information

- The Parliament website contains *Hansard* and the Research Papers produced by the Library Clerks as well as being a mine of other information, www.parliament.co.uk
- The web addresses of the Scottish Parliament, Welsh and Northern Ireland Assemblies are, respectively:
  www.scottish.parliament.uk
  ww.wales.gov.uk and
  www.ni-assembly.gov.uk
- Vacancies in the Westminster Parliament are usually handled by the agency, Capita RAS and advertised on their website www.rasnet.co.uk
- The Library Association, 7 Ridgmount St. London WC1E 7AE. www.la-hq.org.uk

4 The Civil Service – general fast stream

Change is probably not the first word that springs to mind when you think of the Civil Service. Yet, over the past twenty years or so, this vast bureaucracy has undergone radical re-organisation. The Thatcher years of the 1980s saw the introduction of what was called the Next Steps programme which involved, amongst other things, the creation of agencies (the Benefits and Environment Agencies, for example) to deal with the day to day implementation of policy and the delivery of services. Almost three-quarters of the current 460,000 or so civil servants now work in them. Decentralisation of management was subsequently extended by devolving responsibility for most recruitment and pay levels to individual departments. This may seem no big deal to an outsider, but in fact it represented an enormous cultural shift in an organisation hitherto so tightly controlled from the centre.

And the change is set to continue. Constitutional reform, freedom of information and human rights legislation, new technology, greater involvement in Europe and an ever more demanding and less deferential public will see to that. For some, the pace of change will always be too fast, for others too slow. In 1999, just two years into his first term of office, Tony Blair's off the cuff remark about having scars on his back from the fight to introduce change into a reluctant public sector was widely interpreted by those in the know as referring specifically to Whitehall, the main civil service departments of central government not the public sector as a whole.

The call for 'joined-up' government is driving the need to find new ways of working and radical change will inevitably provoke fierce debate. But, such discussion is not merely of academic interest.

Greater emphasis on the efficient delivery of services, closer relationships between departments, more flexible dealings with the private sector, and senior civil servants increasingly acting as managers rather than just policy advisers, will all affect the nature of work in the Civil Service. As job-seekers, you will need to examine your own preconceptions and be prepared to amend them in the face of a changing reality. However, whatever changes do take place, all agree that the 'public service ethos' must remain. Precise definitions of the 'ethos', and the true extent of impartiality, may be debated but the British Civil Service does pride itself on its neutrality and ability to serve the Government of the day whatever its political colour. As a (senior) civil servant you may be able to influence policy, but ultimately you must serve your political masters even when their beliefs and aims are at odds with your own. People with very strong political views may find this hard, if not impossible, to do.

Recruitment

The Civil Service consists of over 60 Departments, more than 100 Agencies and employs about 2% of the working population. Inevitably in an organisation of this size the various parts of it will have slightly different cultures. If you're interested in particular Departments then try and get some work experience arranged. See the Further Information section for contact details.

In terms of permanent recruitment, the main distinction in the Civil Service is between Fast Stream and Main Stream. The former refers to specific work/training schemes on which there are around 250-300 vacancies each year for graduates from a variety of disciplines. Main Stream really means everything else. It covers jobs needing just a few GCSEs to a Senior Manager or scientific officer requiring extensive experience and/or qualifications. The posts profiled in the Main Stream chapter give a taste of the variety and which may be of interest to those seeking a career related to politics. To find out more about the range of opportunities in the Main Stream, keep an eye on the job advertisements in the press, on the Departmental web pages and on the website of Capita RAS which is an employment agency handling many Main Stream vacancies (addresses in the further information sections).

The Fast Stream Development Programme

The Fast Stream Development Programme is the Civil Service equivalent of the commercial sector's graduate training schemes. It is the vehicle through which 'high flyers', i.e. potential senior civil servants of the future, are recruited and trained.

Although in the singular, the title Fast Stream Development Programme is the overall name given to a number of separate graduate recruitment schemes -the General Fast Stream; Economists (other than for the Diplomatic Service; they are recruited through the General Fast Stream); Statisticians; Government Communications Headquarters (GCHQ); and Inland Revenue. Each scheme has its own application procedure.

People who say they 'want to work in politics' are usually attracted to specific areas within the General Fast Stream and so what follows will concentrate on this. If you are interested in the other schemes, you can get more information from the addresses in the further information section.

The General Fast Stream

First, a word about terminology. The name 'General Fast Stream' is used in the annual Recruitment Report, though the recruitment literature itself just uses the title Fast Stream. To add to the confusion, you may well find some people outside the Civil Service still referring to it by its old name of Administrative Fast Stream. A rose by any other name, it's all the same thing, i.e. a challenging programme of work and training to prepare you for promotion.

When applying for the General Fast Stream, there is just one form to complete and you indicate an order of preference from a number of options which include Science and Engineering, Diplomatic Service (Economists) and European Fast Stream (Lawyer). However, the four options which will probably be of most interest are:

1. *Home Civil Service*: Of the 50 or so Departments comprising the Home Civil Service, about 18 recruit fast streamers each year. These include all the main ones such as the Cabinet Office; Home Office; Education and Employment; Health; Culture Media and Sport; Environment; Transport and the Regions; International Development and the territorial offices in Wales, Scotland and Northern Ireland.

The number of vacancies varies slightly from year to year, but has averaged out at 107 over the last four. Likewise, the ratio of applications to places can differ but is generally between 24 and 30 to 1; in 1999 it was 27.7 to 1.

2. Diplomatic Service: The Diplomatic Service is the overseas arm of the Foreign and Commonwealth Office in London and its role 'to protect and promote British interests overseas and to advise and support ministers as they formulate Britain's foreign policy'.

There is considerable competition for the 25 or so places available each year. In 1999, the ratio of applications to places was 63.1, giving an overall success rate of 1.9%. (Fast streamers in the Diplomatic Service are called Policy Entrants.)

3. European Fast Stream (EFS): This element was specifically devised to help UK nationals prepare for a career in one of the EU Institutions. European fast streamers are employed in the Home Civil Service, but their work will be skewed towards EU matters and include a secondment to Brussels. EFSers are encouraged and helped to apply for permanent posts in the EU institutions, but if unsuccessful remain in the Home Civil Service.

Again, the number of vacancies varies but is 10 to 20 per year. The application to places ratio in 1999 was 71 to 1.

4. Clerkships in the Commons and Lords: With normally only 2 or 3 places a year this element of the competition usually has the highest application to places ratio and in 1999 this was 154.5 to 1 for the Commons and 103 to 1 for the Lords. Although recruited through the fast stream process, Clerks are not strictly civil servants but employees of the Houses of Commons and Lords and you will find more information about them and their work in the chapter on Staff of the Parliaments.

These figures on vacancies and applications are not given to depress or deter; but horror stories do abound. Yes, of course there is competition, but no more so than for the 'blue chip' companies.

What do Fast Streamers do?

According to the 1998–9 Annual Recruitment Report, many applicants did not have a terribly clear idea of what being a fast streamer involved even when they were going through the selection process; but that's hardly surprising. One of the major attractions of the programme is the variety it offers. Precisely because of this diversity, there is no simple job description.

The recruitment literature gives interesting, but of necessity comparatively brief, profiles of fast streamers in various departments. More generally, it explains that Home Civil Service fast streamers could be involved in 'researching and analysing policy options...consulting and negotiating with other organisations, developing and managing major projects...supporting Ministers in their parliamentary work and the management of their Departments'. Those in the Diplomatic Service may start as Desk Officers for particular countries '...in touch with relevant missions...and co-ordinating visits by leading dignitaries or UK Ministers.' But what does all this mean on a day-to-day basis? Four gallant fast streamers who had joined between 1997 and 1999, kindly volunteered to keep diaries of three weeks during January to March 2000. Their brief was to record what they did and any personal observations that would give a sense of them as people and not just employees. I think these snapshots give a good insight into the work of fast streamers in various departments (namely Treasury, Diplomatic Service, Ministry of Agriculture Fisheries and Food and International Development) and at different points early on in their careers.

European Fast Stream (EFS): Calum Miller joined the European Fast Stream straight from university in September 1999. He now works in HM Treasury as a policy advisor on international trade. In a gap year between his secondary education in Scotland and taking up a place to study Philosophy, Politics and Economics at Oxford, he worked for Marks and Spencer in Glasgow and as a volunteer teacher in West Bengal.

17–21 January

Mon   *A slow day. Cheered myself up by making some travel arrangements for trip to Geneva. Morning spent on other people's work: commenting on a Department of Trade and Industry (DTI) brief and thinking about a Treasury colleague's paper on investment. After lunch, pinned boss down for a chat about our long-term (i.e. next month's) work programme. Pleased that we set out some clear projects. Drafted a note on last Friday's meeting. Set off at 5.45 for French class* [at a commercial language school]. *One-to-one since Susanna, my fellow EFSer at Ministry of Agriculture, Fisheries and Food, was ill. Tried to describe an organagram of the Treasury. Not many people can do that in English. I certainly can't do it in French.*

Tue   *Overnight, DTI had sent round draft answer to a parliamentary question. Love it when there's work to get on with at 8.40. After that, started preparation for World Trade Organisation (WTO) Trade and Development Committee meeting in Geneva. Have done lots of reading over last two weeks on developing countries and trade, plus various meetings on aspects of that agenda. Question was, where to start . . . Interrupted by call from World Bank consultant. Bit techy for me. Need a real economist. Put together an outline for this piece on development. Finished up in time for leaving drinks for two trade colleagues. Funny how hard it is not to talk about work in a social setting. Slunk away at 7.*

Wed   *Tube was a disaster. Got to French class ten minutes late. Wednesday morning is grammar time (we're too tired to be much use on Monday evenings). Had to run to the office for meeting at 10 which I had arranged (good planning). Helpful discussion with colleagues on handling Biotechnology issues. Biggest benefit was putting faces to names. Had a fun lunch with two other EFSers. Finished off paper on trade and developing countries in the afternoon. EU Free Trade Agreement with South Africa is in the news, so read the (Foreign Office) telegrams for background. Made it to the airport just in time. Met colleagues from Department for International Development (DFID) on their way out of the lounge, having just called me over the tannoy. Smooth flight. Very comfortable hotel.*

Thu   *Busy day of meetings in Geneva. Started at the WTO at 9.00, with a meeting with the Deputy Director General. Not on a topic I know much about, so listened and learnt. Chance to ask a few questions on more general WTO issues at end of meeting. Met the Ghanaian representative in Geneva. Realised the real capacity constraints on developing countries as he described his workload. Working lunch with representatives of 'like-minded' delegations on trade and development. Good food, interesting discussion, but need to practice making mental notes! Afternoon meetings also helpful: one at the UK Mission to the United Nations, one with officials back in the WTO. Felt we had deserved our fondue by the time we got back to the hotel.*

Fri   *Further meetings. Starting to get a feel for how business is done out here. Not quite as the press represent it: the WTO secretariat is very small. Helpful just to see the set-up and the interactions between representatives of the member states and the WTO officials. Impressed friends by turning up for birthday party in London straight from the airport (ah, the life of an international traveller).*

21–25 February

Mon   *Morning – big thoughts. Trying to work out a paper on the 'coherence of international institutions'. Relates to some of the theory I studied at university, but – five months into the job – it looks a bit different 'on the inside'. Spend some time in the library gathering my thoughts (discovered a tranquil corner without phones, e-mails or interruptions – bliss). Afternoon meeting on the environment: colleagues from across Treasury with a range of interests. French class.*

Tue   *Slow day. Spent much of morning looking for some elusive statistics on trade flows and tariff levels for Embassy in Washington. Became very indebted to economically-literate colleague who demonstrated enormous patience. Following up yesterday's meeting, did some 'green' work in the afternoon. The European Commission produced a study on the impacts of trade liberalisation, and had requested feedback on the findings. Took some time to work through the lengthy report.*

Wed   *8.30: Making travel arrangements (French conversation class). 10:30: Making travel arrangements to Sussex University ('real' work). Meeting with senior officials on a second International Development White Paper. Will mean plenty of work for me on the trade and development front. Received Department of Trade and Industry (DTI) briefs for Friday's trade meeting in Brussels: comments duly returned. Talked through my personal objectives with my line manager. Objective number one: leave the office earlier in the evening!* [on average Calum works until around 6.30]

Thu   *We've moved! Trade branch now belongs to a new team. What does this mean? Work. Prepared a list of responsibilities and current issues for meeting with our new team-leader. Only when you put it down on paper that you realise how much we (are supposed to) do. Meeting went well. Came away with a few new responsibilities to add to the list. Spent the afternoon wading through some academic papers on institutional governance and the role of the WTO in preparation for tomorrow's seminar.*

Fri   *A day at the seaside. Left early to get down to Sussex University for a day-long seminar. The Cabinet Office's Performance and Innovation Unit had gathered an interesting selection of participants, from academia, NGOs* [non governmental organisations], *think tanks, and government. Ranged over a number of high-level issues on the institutional reform of the WTO. Not an easy topic, but enjoyed the (relatively) peaceful surroundings.*

27–31 March

Mon   *The first of two days out of the office. Went to Chatham House, home of the Royal Institute of International Affairs, for a conference on 'Trade, Investment and Sustainability'. The organisers had lined up a range of speakers, many concerned with how to make economic growth more compatible with human development and environmentally sustainable behaviour. All interesting, and some of it very relevant to my job. Rushed from there to Department for International Development (DFID) at lunchtime for an afternoon 'round-table'. Government officials heavily outnumbered by academics, so I kept a low profile, and learnt. Then onto French, before resting my over-worked brain.*

Tue   *Back at Chatham House. More panel discussions and interesting speakers. A sense of unreality dawns as I think about taking all of this information and ideas back to my own work. Very daunting: I can't claim to know a fraction of the combined knowledge at this conference when I go to advise ministers. At least there were a few people here who I strongly disagreed with, so not a 100% intimidation rating.*

Wed   *Began the day talking about the French judicial system: slightly unexpected. Further surprises in the office: though I suspected it, nothing could quite prepare me for the groaning e-mail in-box: 98 messages! Tried in vain to sift through these as more arrived. It had been a busy two days in my absence. Discovered I would need to go to Brussels and Bonn next week for meetings on trade and development. Spent the afternoon at the Ministry of Agriculture, Fisheries and Food, listening to a presentation on agricultural*

> commodities. *Back in the office, planned a meeting which I will chair tomorrow. Briefing for the Chancellor of the Exchequer requested by close tomorrow.*

Thu   *Still catching up on those e-mails, and trying to find out what we mean by 'capacity building for development' in preparation for my meetings next week. Over to DFID mid-morning to discuss a draft chapter of a White Paper. Meeting ran for three hours. Grrrr. Not a good day for meetings: my meeting this afternoon was a shambles. The key person failed to turn up, and – as it was on a technical subject – this left the rest of us floundering. Eventually agreed to stop sinking and call it a day. Depressing. Finished the Chancellor's briefing in time, though.*

Fri   *In at 8.15: a new Friday record. Needed to prepare for next week's meetings before an EFS study day. A mistake to go in to the office as I only picked up more work: the Chancellor's office wanted comments on his speaking note. Sat through the first presentation on Enlargement of the EU while reading and amending the note. Back to Treasury in the lunch break to get this off to private office. Still time for a delicious lunch and to catch up with EFSers back from Brussels for the day. Interesting afternoon presentation on Justice and Home Affairs. Adjourned to the pub.*

Diplomatic Service: Eleanor Petch joined the Diplomatic Service in 1998 straight from university. She spent one year as EU Desk Officer for the Western Balkans and EFTA (European Free Trade Association) and since October 1999 has been Desk Officer for Hungary and assistant for Poland. Both these posts have been in London, but her next posting will be overseas. Her degree, from Cambridge, was in English.

24–28 January

Mon   *Started with weekly departmental meeting – briefing on Head of Department's recent travel to the Baltics and all staff giving run down of important events in their diaries this week. Discussion of key issues (and department lottery syndicate!). Lots of phoning today – chasing leads on different visit programmes we are organising, to confirm dates and Hungarian visitors. Discuss with my opposite number at the Home Office and at Post how to finalise the text of the Memorandum of Understanding on Organised Crime for Hungarian ministerial visit to UK in February.* [Embassies and staff abroad are known as 'Post'; in this case the officer dealing with Justice and Home Affairs issues in the British Embassy in Budapest.] *Finalise several pieces of written work on export licences which are required before certain types of goods, like arms, can be sent abroad. Also work on MPs' correspondences. This means drafting ministerial replies to issues or questions raised by MPs on behalf of their constituents. In my department property restitution matters in Poland crop up quite regularly.*

    pm: Spoke to a group of new entrants about the benefits of joining the Diplomatic Service Association (my trade union – I have been on the committee for a year).

Tue   *Lots of bitty separate pieces of work. Phone calls with tight deadlines for information and some interesting research on protocol for signing of Memoranda of Understanding. I also spoke to the commercial section at Post and British Trade International in London about the Opportunity Hungary Trade campaign. Our Director, Stephen Wright (Director = senior official – one above a head of department) is visiting Budapest at the end of the month and today I started compiling papers for his visit.*

pm: Asked for advice from my line manager and deputy head of department about a tricky constituency letter, before drafting a reply to the MP. Later phoned several posts to discuss jobs in posting round for my grade; bids due next week. [A list of jobs available is circulated and each fast streamer can put in a 'bid', i.e. a request, for their top 5. The final decision is made by the Postings Board.]

Train late again – commuting into London is a real disadvantage of working in Whitehall.

Wed   *Very busy. Last minute briefing call for a meeting between Mr Vaz* [Minister of State] *and an executive from Tescos took up most of the day. I rescheduled other work around this, but phone doesn't stop ringing with other queries and requests.*

pm: Investigated possible departmental backing for various assistance projects costing up to £120,000 – all good publicity for HMG [Her Majesty's Government] *and worthwhile, but we can't do everything. Meeting with Personnel manager to discuss posting choices. Weighed up pros and cons of different posts from hard language training opportunities to climate. Lots to think about before Monday.*

Thu   *Walked down Millbank to the Diplomatic Service Language Centre for the lunchtime beginners' Spanish class – great fun. Took collated briefing pack to Director and attended meeting with the Hungarian Ambassador to run over issues for Director's visit to Budapest– some interesting topics on EU and visits which I will follow up tomorrow. Departmental tea break every Thursday is a great opportunity to have a chat. Then I had time to catch up on the telegram float (documents distributed around the office electronically) from this morning.*

Fri   *Attended Home Office briefing for London Ambassadors on the implications of the new Immigration and Asylum bill. I don't know much about this topic – it was organised by a colleague who is an expert in this field. Useful to meet the Consul General from Hungarian Embassy. At lunchtime I went to a choir rehearsal (FCO choir sings at various functions including the Christmas party and Remembrance Day ceremony). Finalised briefing for Director's visit next week and spoke to Post on various issues. I probably discuss almost every significant piece of work with Post at some stage. Since my visit in December I know most people there and can phone and chat to them about individual cases and general news.*

14–18 February

Mon   *Returned from leave today to a pile of papers in my intray. Most urgent was a written Parliamentary Question (PQ) for the House of Lords – only a short time to write it, but nevertheless a good opportunity to publicise work we are doing in Hungary. Most of the day was spent going to or organising meetings. Weekly departmental meeting was a bit thin on the ground due to people travelling. It included general reminders about IT and the department's replies to Ambassadors' Annual Reviews which haven't gone out yet.* [All British ambassadors write a review of the previous year in their countries.] *Finally, the Organised Crime Memorandum of Understanding was signed by the Home Secretary during the Hungarian Minister's visit last week. We can now use an agreed text and continue all the good work in that area. Glad that all concerned were pleased with the visit (the first I had organised).*

Tue   *Often I arrive at work determined to get one or two pieces of work done and then get overtaken by other tasks. Today I discovered that I will be taking a lead in organising talks between the Foreign Secretary and Central European Foreign Ministers at the end of the month – a good learning experience. This morning I spent time looking at some longer term aims such as training and development courses and appraisal objectives. I hope that the office will send me on an intermediate management course as I already line-manage one member of support staff and will be responsible for others when I go abroad. Lunch with my mentor today (I have been paired with someone from another part of the Foreign Office) who was able to give me good, impartial advice on postings and objective setting, as well as a friendly chat. It is always useful to get a different perspective by discussing things outside the department.*

Wed   *Quieter day in the office as my line manager was away in Brussels. Several enquiries from members of the public, covering passports and travel advice.* [Calls from the public sometimes get referred from the general switchboard.] *These are not specific policy issues so they were directed to our Consular Division. Most of the day was spent on the intricacies of ministerial visits. A major briefing exercise is underway for the Foreign Secretary before he sees his counterparts from Central Europe. We are also planning ahead for other ministers and senior officials involved in our region. Union committee meeting this lunchtime – discussion included long hours, Working Time Directive and pay review round.*

Thu   *Very busy day preparing background briefing for a speech by Mr Vaz and collating briefing for other meetings. Hindered by an office IT system which seems to obstruct rather than help interdepartmental communication, but an email system should soon be installed throughout the office. A very sociable afternoon. I was departmental tea monitor this Thursday – it is really nice to chat to people from the whole department – although of course we always end up talking about work! Later I went to a leaving party for a friend who is about to start language training before going to Japan. No word from my postings board today – but maybe I will hear something tomorrow.*

Fri   *The main focus of today was lunch at the Hungarian Embassy with my Head of Section, Head of Department, the Hungarian Ambassador and his Deputy and another senior Hungarian diplomat. This was an excellent opportunity to run over different topics in a more relaxed and informal setting. I am still getting used to 'dining' etiquette – the hardest thing is trying to listen, take notes and eat simultaneously. We came back with lots of queries to follow up next week. Personnel rang to say that it is virtually certain I got my first choice (Prague) at the postings board, so I am very pleased. This will mean about 10 months of language training – a fantastic opportunity. I took the opportunity to head home a bit early as it has been a busy week – flexible hours make it possible to vary working hours sometimes. This weekend I am back in the office to take part in a crisis exercise – I have volunteered to staff a desk in the Emergency Unit for a day while the office tests its emergency procedures – should be very interesting.* [This unit is a communications centre which can be set up for 24 hour working in the event of an emergency. The Desk Officer for the geographical area involved takes the lead and is assisted by other volunteers such as Eleanor]

27–31 March

Mon   *Short departmental meeting. I attended a call by the visiting Hungarian parliamentary speaker on Mr. Vaz (I wrote the briefing for this meeting last week). It was a diplomatically useful courtesy call, but did not include a great deal of detailed policy discussion – I will now have to write up the call for the record. Later I met the visiting parliamentary delegation at a discussion session with academics and MPs organised by an NGO (non-governmental organisation) which is active in our region. It was useful to hear lots of different points of view and reactions to the official, and off the record opinions expressed. I got caught in a downpour on the way back and arrived back in the office very wet.*

        p.m.: Very busy with briefing for Mr Vaz's ministerial conference this weekend. Lots of paperwork to wade through after my day off last Friday.

Tue   *More representational work [i.e. representing the Department externally] today with a lunch and an evening lecture to attend. Such networking is always valuable, but it is a real balancing act to decide how much time it is sensible to spend away from the office – the paper pile does not get any smaller. Lunch at the Inter-Parliamentary Union with the Hungarian visiting delegation was very interesting as MPs do not always have to tow the government line when they are talking to foreign visitors. On a personal note – I have not yet quite mastered the diplomatic skill of eating food I do not like in order to avoid offending my hosts. This evening's lecture was useful. Didn't get home until 9.30pm.*

Wed   *Lots of competing deadlines. Everyone in the section is very busy – we try to help each other out as much as possible, to get all the work done. Time pressures often mean that background work like reading piles up and it can be a struggle to keep it under control – this evening I hacked away at it so I can start with a clearer desk tomorrow.*

Thu   *Busy day of very short deadlines, preparing briefing and programme details for the conference delegations which arrive tomorrow. Also spent some time speaking to the Diplomatic Service Language Centre and Training Wing about pre-posting training to organise my courses and full time language training. An oral PQ on Hungary arrived for me to prepare. Oral (as opposed to written) parliamentary questions require lots and lots of briefing as a wide range of topics have to be covered for all the possible supplementary questions. This afternoon we were making final preparations for tomorrow's meetings and press conference and considering urgent deadlines for early next week. I had a chat with the Administrative Assistant who I line manage about future prospects and her impressions of her current job. This evening I went to an Embassy reception – more new contacts (both from overseas and other government departments/NGOs) – another late night.*

Fri   *A successful day. Shepherded visiting Central European ministers to and from press conferences this morning. The weekend conference seems to have got off to a good start. Lunch with my mentor was very relaxed as we discussed my future plans and useful contacts. This afternoon the section was decimated due to the conference and various other trips. I had to complete a very fast turnaround on a briefing for the Secretary of State for a meeting next week and then I made an attack on my overflowing intray. Now I have locked up all the cupboards and I'm off to a party.*

Ministry of Agriculture, Fisheries and Food: Judicaelle Hammond writes from the Meat Hygiene Division of the Ministry of Agriculture, Fisheries and Food (MAFF). Of dual nationality and bi-lingual (French and English), Judicaelle did her Baccalaureate in France, a first degree in Politics at Queen Mary and Westfield College, London and a Master of Arts in European Politics and Administration at the College of Europe. Her MA dissertation was entitled 'The BSE crisis: policy failure in multi-level governance.' Immediately before joining the Civil Service Judicaelle had undertaken a stage (work placement) at the European Commission.

Judicaelle's role is to review, develop, and help implement European Union (EU) and domestic regulations on (red) meat hygiene which covers the inspection of production plants and the hygiene charged for fresh meat.

24–28 January

Awfully busy week, but I prefer it this way.

Mon   *New Head of Division starts today; may make a difference to management style and policy approach. Watch this space. Helped prepare the Government's reply to the recent report on red tape in the meat sector. Minister due to make an announcement at the National Farmer's Union Conference, so high profile and requires briefing.*

Wed   *An MP has written to Minister of State, requesting a meeting. Researched the constituent's case, put briefing together as well as a draft reply for the Minister's signature. Commented on internal consultation on the future communication strategy of the Food Standards Agency.*

Thu   [Judicaelle will be referring to two pieces of legislation regarding meat hygiene rules but as she cannot mention them by name, will call them A and B.] *Unexpected problem. One of the Department of Health Ministers due to sign our new legislation 'A' before it goes to Parliament has raised a number of fundamental questions. Commissioned (short) briefing from 3 sources and started my own bit.*

Fri   *I had said short briefing. From one provider I got 21 pages of rules, no reference to their applicability in our case. I know the staff are new, but still, this means me hassling* someone more senior, which is a waste of their time and mine.

Discussed with my manager a draft letter to our Attaché at the Paris Embassy, about abattoir subsidy allegations, published in a Belgian newspaper. Letter changed and dispatched.

Started proofreading proposed legislation 'B' (colleague in charge on leave); deeply boring and requiring maximum concentration, but essential.

One more crisis: briefing for legislation 'B' did not get to Department of Health (Minister's signature needed). Emailed it sharpish and informed various key colleagues.

Next week chock-full of meetings, some for networking, some about change coming with the advent of the Food Standards Agency.

7–11 February

Mon   Frantic checks that everything is OK on legislative front. That and finalising letter informing the industry of the change and drafting news release took up most of the day. Unproductive, if enjoyable, buzz of activity.

Tue   Relief – legislation 'A' and 'B' laid before Parliament (just). Will come into force on date planned unless some MPs call a debate. No time for celebration though; guidance on how to enforce the legislation still needs to be finalised.

Had to re-write large chunks of press release on advice from my manager. Does not feel right. My experience at the EU Commission Spokesman's Service tells me it is far too long and detailed.

Examined letter from firm of solicitors on claim for compensation [for erroneous advice given by Department some years previous]. Does not contain any of the evidence I had asked for. Contacted Legal Department about way forward (in my view no evidence = no money).

Wed   Day spent on guidance on the enforcement of legislation 'A'. Will have to talk to Veterinary Adviser about practicalities. Also worked on another long-running project; must be finished by end of the month to go out to consultation and on website.

Thu   Spent morning guinea-pigging at a management workshop for senior civil servants in South West London. Awful weather, nice houses. Got lost and soaked on the way, but got there on time. Interviewed on what motivates me etc. by one woman and four men. Tried to project enthusiastic, bright, pro-active image, but gave straight answers, because I might work for them one day. Nice lunch, gossip about previous Ministers (perks of the job).

Back to the office pm. As expected, Head of Division thinks press release is too long. Back to square one. Pulled out improved original version and tried again. Much better response. Circulated draft for comments.

Fri   Job description for potential next posting has arrived. Soul searching time. Talked to various people. Sounds interesting, challenging and different from my current job but 1) suitable for me? 2) can secondment to Food Standards Agency be arranged?

More work on several projects. Nothing too exciting, though every time one problem is solved another seems to emerge.

27–31 March

Mon   *Last week in my current job. Decided to press on with the secondment to the Food Standards Agency and the transfer was confirmed last week. This week will be devoted to tidying up all the loose ends. As I am not being replaced, several people will have to finish the projects I was working on.*

     Revised guidance notes on legislation 'A' following the meeting I organised on Friday 24 (about 20 attendees. Worst instance of slurred speech in months, due mainly to tiredness.).

Tue   *Packed up my first box of belongings. Hopefully it will arrive at my new desk before I do. Started a list of tasks to complete for whoever takes over my projects. Drafted and sent a minute requesting briefing on the debt recovery procedure applicable in England and Wales, compared to that in Scotland. Wrote down my job description, work and development objectives, recent training etc. for my final probation report. Que sera, sera. I am both reasonably confident and still nervous.*

     Short meeting with my line manager and others to discuss the briefing requested by the Chief Executive of the Food Standards Agency (FSA) in advance of the FSA's launch (to be ready by 10:00 on Thursday). Submitted comments and suggestions on a MAFF document on the Modernising Government reform. Looks like things are going to change, mainly for the better.

Wed   *Packed box No. 2. Drafted briefing for the Chief Executive. Watched video of extract of 'Countryfile' on the problems in the meat sector. Tried to catch senior colleagues before they travelled off to Brussels, to clarify a few points on proposed amendments to a piece of meat hygiene legislation.*

     Last minute work on a draft application form and guidance leaflet, which should go out for public consultation as I leave. Continued list of remaining tasks, making sure the colleagues likely to be involved know where to find files, records, drafts etc.

Thu   *Packed box No. 3, the last one. Finished my list of remaining tasks, with detailed explanation where necessary. Started delivering files with a broad grin and my best 'wicked-witch-of-the-East' laugh to some innocent colleagues. Reactions ranged from 'what have you been doing for the past 9 months?' (I could have done without your interesting work, thank you very much), to 'you'll be missed' (pass me the hankies, quick), via 'of course, you are leaving next week!' (surprise and horror). Passed on any documents held electronically to the relevant colleagues, emptied my email folders, printed the documents sent by my next boss as an advance warning of the issues to come.*

Fri   *Coincidentally it's the last day in MAFF for most of my colleagues. The Head of Division has decided to mark the occasion with a drink in the afternoon. Three people are leaving the Division, including me. Arrived loaded with food, found a clean desk, dumped it all, and started on my very last pieces of work and tidying up.*

     I will look back on this posting with a bit of nostalgia, I suspect. It has provided me with plenty of challenges and intellectual stimulation. I was given opportunities to try my hand at a wide variety of tasks. My management invested a lot of time into training me up, and took risks by delegating to me. I hope it paid off for them; it certainly was a very worthwhile experience for me. Staff at all levels were very nice to work with, and proved commendably tolerant of my chocolate cravings, residual galli-

cisms and propensity to statements like: 'I could have sworn I saw it somewhere'...Time to borrow the Divisional corkscrew.

Department for International Development: Laurie Lee is the most experienced of the four diarists and the only one to be currently working overseas. He studied politics at Nottingham and joined the Fast Stream in 1997. Before that, he spent 10 months working in the House of Commons for MPs Keith Hill and Yvette Cooper (both Labour) either side of the 1997 General Election. His first post at the Department for International Development (DFID) was in the Policy Planning Unit of the Central Aid Policy and Resources Department. The main areas of work were: co-ordination of DFID's input into UK Presidency of G8; Ministerial briefing and Parliamentary work; secretariat for the Inter-Departmental Ministerial Working Group on Development; monitoring implementation of the 1997 International Development White Paper.

In September 1998 he took up his current two-year post in DFID Southern Africa (DFIDSA). DFIDSA is a regional office, covering the Southern Africa Customs Union countries; Botswana, Lesotho, Namibia, South Africa and Swaziland. The total annual development assistance programme is £45 million, most of it going to South Africa. The Pretoria office consists of 23 UK-based staff and 31 staff appointed in-country, and it is from there that Laurie records two weeks in January and February. Though perhaps not typical weeks, they give an insight into the type of work that may be undertaken as fast streamers advance in their careers.

17–21 January

Mon *10.00. Weekly office meeting to touch base with each other and exchange information. Occasionally feels like a chore, but is an important fixture. Unless travelling, all operational staff attend plus some of the support staff (usually 20+ in total). A representative from the British High Commission also usually attends and today mentioned the planned visit of Peter Hain, Foreign Office Minister for Africa (among other things), at the end of the month. Important that Mr Hain gets a feel for DFID's activities in South Africa. DFID's Internal Audit Unit (IAU), who arrived today for two weeks, explained why they were here and what they will be doing. Their remit is to see that we are spending taxpayers' money effectively (achieving our own objectives) and properly (according to the rules).*

Main task today is revision of the programme for the International Development Parliamentary Select Committee's (IDC) visit next month, based on comments from colleagues in DFIDSA, the High Commission, the Consulate-General in Johannesburg, and in London, on a draft I circulated last week. Committee will consider the programme again tomorrow.

It is my new assistant's second week in DFID. After an intensive and rather theoretical five days of general induction last week, am trying to give her some specific tasks to get her teeth into. It is the first time I have had full management responsibility for another member of staff and an exciting challenge.

Tue   a.m.: My assistant and I had a long conversation with one of the IAU team looking at DFIDSA's 'pre-Implementation' procedures; i.e. the stages before a project becomes operational. He wanted to know how we went about producing a Country Strategy Paper for South Africa and ensuring that (in particular) new initiatives are consistent with that policy framework. I found it interesting to verbalise this for someone outside the immediate office. Also useful background for my new assistant.

Rest of the day: routine paperwork and guiding my assistant through procedures on two of our projects.

Wed   9.00: My boss or I attend the High Commission weekly meeting (also attended by military, commercial and cultural officers from the British missions in Pretoria and Johannesburg). We discussed various planned (and cancelled) visits to, and from, the UK. European Development Commissioner is in Pretoria trying to break through the latest deadlock on the EU-South Africa Trade, Development and Co-operation Agreement, but there was no read-out yet (we will hopefully get one from the next bi-monthly EU Development Officials Meeting at the Portuguese Embassy – they have the Presidency-next week). Afterwards met separately with my counterparts in the High Commission and Consulate-General on the IDC visit; but as no feedback yet from the Committee's Clerk in London, we couldn't go much further.

p.m.: Assistant and I discussed her Annual Performance and Development Plan (objectives and success criteria). Will keep revising this throughout the year as she grows into what is also a new post in the office. A useful opportunity to talk with her about how things are going so far and to clarify the purpose of her three month probationary period. I reassured her that I would give plenty of warning if she was not meeting the requirements so that we could address any problems constructively together. In return, she would have to tell me if she was having problems, or if I wasn't giving her sufficiently challenging work. We agreed that we need to be open and frank with each other.

Thu   a.m.: Feedback from the Clerk of the IDC late last night, so this morning had another look at their programme and divided up responsibilities more precisely between ourselves and colleagues in High Commissions in Pretoria and Cape Town and Consulate-General in Johannesburg.

12.30: A farewell at the High Commission for two friends was also an opportunity to catch up with (and introduce my assistant to) a few South African contacts. Not a typical diplomatic do, of which I probably average about one a week, varying from small dinners to large receptions. These are much improved if either (a) you know there are people there you want to meet or (b) you know there are people there you have already met (and want to meet again). However, occasionally you do meet someone interesting who you didn't expect to be there and that's even better.

Fri   *08.30. Head of Department and I met briefly with half-a-dozen advisers (our technical experts on health, education etc.) and administrators (the rest of us) to discuss latest revisions to the IDC's programme. I will give the Clerk another revised programme on Monday, for the Committee's next meeting, on Tuesday.*

09.00: Different group of us met with GTZ, the German technical assistance implementation agency, to exchange notes on our programmes in South Africa, in particular to discuss the possibility of co-ordinating our activities around new sustainable livelihoods programmes in the poorest, often rural, areas (I will be going to Eastern Cape next week to discuss these ideas further with the Provincial Government there). I gave an overall introduction to our Country Strategy and ways of working and colleagues then got into the detail of their own sectors; more useful background for my assistant.

11.30: Chaired a Project Concept Note (PCN) meeting with about 10 members of the office. One of the IAU team also sat in, because considering a project as a concept is an important part of the pre-implementation procedures before we progress to full design. A network of local NGOs (non-governmental organisations) presented their proposals for strengthening the civil society sector in South Africa; I chaired the subsequent discussion. Advisers are increasingly asking me to act as the neutral chair of such meetings. This seems to work well and is also good experience for me.

p.m.: Clearing correspondence and updating our Country Strategy Implementation Plan, following a meeting last week.

13–18 February

Sun   *07.30. Early start to the week. My boss, myself and a British High Commission representative, met the IDC and two of their Clerks at Cape Town International Airport.*

After breakfast at the hotel, the Clerks and one Member trekked up Table Mountain with us, while the others either went to explore the sights of the Cape or polished off constituency work they had brought with them. Useful to meet the Committee socially before taking them into meetings.

A new variable has arisen. Half the Committee were supposed to be going onto Mozambique after South Africa, but Maputo has been severely flooded. We now have at least three contingency plans…

Mon   *09.00: Official visit starts with political background briefing from the High Commissioner. It is clear from their questions that the Members each have their own particular interests, over and above the Committee's terms of reference for the visit.*

10.00: Committee splits into two groups as we cross the road to Parliament. Group one meets the Trade and Industry, and Finance Committees while I take group two to meet the Committees on Public Service and Administration, Safety and Security, and Labour, to discuss constraints to investment.

11.30: Last minute addition to the Programme; the Health Committee have asked to meet our visitors. Health, including HIV, is an important issue which we have already included in the programme for Johannesburg. But hard to decline and, although time is too tight for an in-depth discussion, I take group two to meet them.

12.30: Lunch with some opposition MPs and academics goes well; again pressed for time and have to skip dessert.

14.00: Group two visit a micro-enterprise training centre which DFID is supporting. I take group one to a Community Safety Pilot Project in the Cape Flats townships. The Committee are particularly impressed with the youth of some of the people trying to tackle crime in their communities.

17.00: Meeting with the South African Education Minister. He is 'a politician's politician' and goes down well with the MPs. He also thanks DFID for its assistance to his department.

18.00: Day officially ends with a well-attended reception at the High Commissioner's residence. MPs meet some interesting people and I catch up with some contacts, who I'll see again next month.

20.00: Return to hotel and, after a well-earned drink, the Committee splits along party lines; we take half of them out to dinner while the others sensibly get an early night. In the bar, I ask the Members and Clerks how they think the day has gone. They agreed that it was full and had been necessary to split into two groups. One member disagreed; she wondered what she'd missed.

Tue   *06.30: Check out of hotel to catch the 08.00 flight to Johannesburg.*

10.50: Arrive at first destination early and my contact isn't there but it gives the Members a chance to look at the new market in downtown Johannesburg. Then, after visiting urban renewal projects in the centre, we go to the Consulate-General's office for a trade/business background briefing. This got a bit technical and the Committee asked our contacts to keep it simple; they wanted the political issues.

15.00: Afternoon was split again, meeting various business and government people to discuss the private sector and development. These meetings provoked some of the best debates of the visit.

17.30: Another reception, for business, media and NGO contacts, all of whom are mainly based in Johannesburg. Another good turn out. With seven MPs, the guests stood a good chance of meeting at least one of them. I took most of the Committee for dinner afterwards.

Wed   *08.00. Presentation over breakfast on the social and legal impact of HIV/AIDS. Perhaps not the best subject for breakfast, but we had to fit it in before today's visit.*

09.30: We depart in two minibuses for Carletonville, south of Johannesburg, where DFID is supporting an AIDS prevention programme among sexworkers and mineworkers.

12.30: After a general introduction from the various project partners, I cut away with two Members for high level calls in Pretoria. The rest of the Committee carry on to the mine sites themselves.

14.00: Meeting with the head of the SA Revenue Service, with whom DFID has its largest project in South Africa. The Committee Chair is impressed and the meeting runs over time.

15.00: Slightly late for a meeting at the Department of Trade and Industry with the official in charge of Trade with Africa. As well as discussing regional issues, he updates us on the latest compromise negotiated with the EU, and South Africa's position on Seattle (WTO meeting in 1999) and a new WTO (World Trade Organisation) trade round.

16.00: Finish the afternoon at the Central Reserve Bank, at the top of the tallest building in Pretoria, meeting one of the Deputy Governors. The Members have been asking lots of questions about macroeconomic policy, interest rates and inflation, and they get some good answers here.

19.30: Dinner at their hotel in Pretoria, mainly with contacts from Government. I'm pleased that Department of Finance make it, as it is the budget next week. We spread the Members around five tables and from the sound of it, they all found some interesting people to talk to.

Thu   *08.00: Second breakfast briefing on AIDS, this time on its economic impact, from an international authority on the subject whom we couldn't get at any other time! Touched some controversial issues and I think the Clerk will want to pursue the contact as the Committee are considering doing a report specifically on HIV/AIDS.*

09.30:Depart the hotel for a small local airfield where group one will be leaving South Africa for Zambia while my boss and I will take the others to KwaZulu Natal in a little ten-seater plane with barely enough room for the luggage. Still not sure if the Mozambique leg of the trip is on.

12.00: Arrive in KwaZulu Natal and spend the afternoon visiting small enterprise support projects. Nearly half of South Africa's population is rural so it is good to get the Committee out of the cities. Also a welcome ease in the pace after a hectic three days; there is even time for a quick swim before dinner.

We get word that the Committee can continue to Mozambique, via Swaziland, if things don't get worse. But if more rain comes, they won't be able to visit anywhere beyond Maputo. The Committee decides to take the risk.

Fri   *09.00. Leave our guest house and head north towards the rain and Duku Duku Forest, where DFID is assisting government to resettle a community living in this forest without any basic amenities.*

10.00: After a formal welcome, we are taken to see the forest. However, the heavy rain has left the tracks difficult for ordinary vehicles and we get stuck in the mud briefly before returning to the forestry station. This turns out to be a blessing in disguise, as it gives the Members plenty of time to talk with the local community representatives. They say that malaria is a bigger threat than AIDS, and show us plans for the new settlement which will be built for them with a school, clinic and other services. It is a good finale to the Committee's visit.

17.00: At the border we hand over the Committee to our Swaziland programme manager who has travelled down from the regional office in Pretoria. We say our goodbyes and head home, wondering what their report will say, but confident that we have put every effort into making the visit a success.

Variety at the heart of government

The diaries illustrate well the diversity of work within and between different departments in the Civil Service and the range of skills needed by fast streamers. So how do the selectors find the right people?

Entry Requirements: The minimum academic requirement is a lower second class honours degree in any discipline, though this requirement may be waived if you have a disability that has prevented you from taking a degree or if you are a serving civil servant applying through the In-Service nomination scheme. In addition, applicants for the European Fast Stream should normally have an 'A' level (or equivalent) in another European Union official language. Having said that, you can still apply if you are bilingual or for some other reason have a high level of language skill but no paper qualification but your linguistic ability might be tested before you are offered a place. The Diplomatic Service does not actually require a qualification in a foreign language, but you will be tested on your aptitude for learning languages.

Regarding age, the European Fast Stream has an upper limit of 41 in order to comply with EU institutions' regulations. The other options do not stipulate a maximum, but as the normal Civil Service retirement age is 60 applicants should have a 'reasonable number of working years' ahead of them. On average in 1997 and 1998 (the latest years for which figures are available at the time of writing) approximately 25% of successful applicants were 21 or under; 50% between 22 and 25; 18% between 26 and 30; and 6% between 31 and 35. For anyone over forty though, there is still some hope – in 1998 a 42 year old was recruited.

Most posts are only open to UK nationals and the Diplomatic Service requires applicants to be British citizens. If you hold dual nationality you may need to check that your 'other half' is acceptable. All applicants for the Diplomatic Service will also be subject to security vetting, but previous mainstream political activity is no bar to entry to any of these General Fast Stream options.

The General Fast Stream Application Procedure This consists of three elements:

Application from: Application forms are available from the agency Capita RAS (address in Further Information section) or, if you're a current student, from your university careers service. There are two closing dates, September and January (to start work the following summer). You can apply by either date for all the options except the Diplomatic Service which requires applications in September. Any job offer made to final year students will be conditional on their degree results.

The application form is pretty straightforward and is only checked for academic and nationality requirements. The first major hurdle is the Qualifying Test (QT). Blind and partially sighted applicants are automatically exempt from the QT and those with other disabilities that may affect their performance can apply for exemption on the application form. If granted, you will be invited to attend a preliminary interview board instead which tests the same job related aptitudes.

Qualifying test: The QT may be computer-based in the future, but at present it is a day-long session held at 29 centres nationwide and consisting of cognitive (aptitude) tests and a biodata test. The latter is more akin to a personality questionnaire and looks at social and transferable skills, motivation, etc. You can't really prepare for this one. However, there are a number of ways you can 'limber up' for the cognitive tests which assess your verbal, numerical and critical reasoning skills.

Before the QT you will automatically be sent a short test familiarisation booklet. There is also a self-assessment package downloadable from the fast stream website (see Further Information). As well as including a self-selection questionnaire to help you decide if the fast stream is for you, this gives examples of test questions for you to assess your performance. If you can't access the internet, then contact Capita RAS for a self-assessment disk.

There is an ever increasing number of books about test-taking and even though the questions may not be exactly the same format as the Civil Service tests, doing them will still give you a valuable mental workout. If you are at university, take advantage of any practice aptitude sessions offered by your careers service. Doing tests under strict exam conditions is good experience. There is some debate about how much you can actually improve your performance by practice, but it's certain that familiarising yourself with the format of these tests will lessen your anxiety and may help to speed up your responses. Time pressure is a crucial factor in all aptitude tests.

The fast stream tests are undoubtedly some of the toughest in graduate recruitment though, and around 90% of applicants get weeded out at the QT stage. If you do make it through, the next step is the Civil Service Selection Board (CSSB – pronounced 'sizbee', to rhyme with frisbee).

CSSB: 'Exhausting but stimulating' was how one CSSB participant described it, and most people who have been through it would probably agree. It is two days of interviews plus group and individual exercises designed to test for the skills required by fast streamers.

Appropriately enough, it takes place just down the road from Whitehall and Westminster in Dean Bradley House. On the first day, all candidates are assigned to groups of 5 which you will stay in for the duration apart from during written exercises. But, you will not be assessed against each other; one, some, all or none of you may pass, depending on your own individual performance.

Each group of 5 candidates is allocated to a panel of three assessors comprising two experienced civil servants and a psychologist According to a spokesperson from the Cabinet Office, the psychologist's role is to take "the lead in gathering and interpreting evidence from fellow assesors on a candidate's personal qualities and potential for self development." Don't worry, you won't be psychoanalysed.Your abilities and aptitudes in three broad areas – people skills, personal skills and task skills – will be tested. For example, the assessors will be looking at how sensitive you are to others, how persuasive you can be, when you can produce ideas and solve problems, how adaptable and resilient you are, etc.The exact nature of the elements in the CSSB may change slightly from year to year but will include a series of individual interviews; exercises designed to test your ability to take in and prioritise large amounts of complex information before reaching conclusions or taking decisions; and, finally, group discussions around various given scenarios. Applicants to the European Fast Stream will also sit a short exam on their knowledge of European affairs, and those going for the Diplomatic Service will be given a verbal language aptitude test. If you are invited to the CSSB, you will receive a booklet beforehand giving detailed information about all the elements involved.

So what sort of people do they really want?: White, male, middle class, Oxbridge? In 1999, just 18% of senior civil servants were women and only 1.6% were from ethnic minorities. The two universities of Oxford and Cambridge account for something over 40% of successful General Fast Stream applicants each year. You could count the number of 'new' university (i.e. ex–Polytechnic) fast streamers on your fingers, and women still make up less than 50% of the annual intake. On the face of it then, the old stereotype seems to hold true.

Recently, however, the powers that be in the Civil Service have been at pains to counteract the image and the reality. Targets have been set to redress the imbalance in the upper echelons and applications for high level posts are encouraged from those outside the public sector and from a range of backgrounds. Fast Stream recruitment literature now emphasises the importance of 'diversity' in terms of gender, race and disability and the Diplomatic Service, amongst others, has launched various initiatives to encourage more applications from ethnic minority candidates.

But the bottom line will always be, 'is the candidate right for the job'? Does s/he have the appropriate mix of qualities — analytical ability, interpersonal skills and political judgement — to develop into a top policy maker and manager? Social background is, of course, an important factor in every individual's educational and personal development and may help or hinder their prospects in any career area. Some people might also argue that each organisation has a particular ethos and will always recruit in its own image. Be that as it may, there does seem to be a genuine willingness to reassess selection procedures in the light of changing roles and work environments. The whole process is continually under review and independent advisers have been appointed.

Each year university careers advisers are invited to observe the CSSB and when I watched 5 hopefuls going through it, there was no doubt in my mind that the treatment of the candidates was equitable and impartial. The assessors were conscientious and scrupulous in their deliberations and the interviews and exercises seemed challenging but fair. The university attended or qualification gained was not relevant; it was how the candidate performed on the day that counted. Indeed, when I observed the process, there was just one candidate in the group who passed and he was not from Oxbridge. My diary of the two days might illustrate why, as well as giving an additional insight into the experience of CSSB. (To ensure anonymity, all the names and some biographical and other details have been changed.)

CSSB Diary: *Dean Bradley House is only 5 minutes away from Parliament, but is itself an unprepossessing office building, its entrance unobtrusively set in a row of small shops.*

Two floors up and you come to the 'common room' – you know it is from the paper sign stuck on the door. Inside the tension is palpable. Forty or so candidates, male and female, in dark suits, clutch cups of coffee and try to make conversation. The receptionist directs me to another room where my panel are based.

The Chair is Michael Summers, a retired DTI official. He joined the civil service in his mid-thirties having previously worked for Rolls Royce and trained as an engineer. The Departmental Assessor is Susan Midwinter. Previously a Clerk in the House of Commons (which as she pointed out is not strictly civil service but a Servant of the House) she now does CSSBs on a consultancy basis; ditto the psychologist, Dennis Platt.

Introductions and coffee out of the way, I am handed a file of papers – all of which will be shredded at the end of the Board. The main items are the application forms of the five candidates allocated to this panel. Unusually, so I am told, this is an all-male group.

Richard Cuff is at Oxford; at 24 is the oldest and the only one pursuing graduate studies. His academic record is formidable, as is that of John Fraser, another Oxford man. Alan Hall is the third Oxbridge candidate, though unlike the other two he is at Cambridge and studying science. Martin Dale is at Kent reading politics and has a reasonable clutch of GCSEs and A levels. The least impressive on paper is Gordon Downes from a not very well-known college in Scotland now studying public policy after a one-year false start on a degree in another subject.

While the candidates are being welcomed and briefed in the common room, Michael, Susan and Dennis give a verbal summary of the application forms of those candidates on which they are 'leading', i.e. those they are responsible for writing up at the end of the board. Richard has put the Diplomatic Service as first choice but it is pointed out that he has very little overseas experience. As well as the Diplomatic and Home Civil Service, Alan wants to be considered for Security. Martin has only one reference (his other, a prominent Labour MP for whom he worked as a researcher, has not yet replied) and none of John's have arrived. Gordon has not made it clear on his form whether the subjects he lists are A levels or highers.

At 10.15 the five candidates appear with cardboard place names which they put on the table in front of them. After a brief welcome by Michael they start the half-hour leaderless discussion on a given topic. John jumps in first and seems to take over but Richard soon chimes in. Alan and Martin both contribute, though not too effectively. Gordon hangs back. His contributions, when they come, are good, but there's not enough of them.

During the discussion the assessors are writing copious notes at a furious pace. At the end of the 30 minutes when jackets have been removed and much water drunk, the first group exercise is over. The candidates leave and move on to a two-hour policy exercise which involves reading and analysing large amounts of information to come up with a policy recommendation.

The panel work in silence for a few minutes, getting their notes and thoughts together.

When the discussion gets under way it is obvious why there was such a furious scribbling of notes. The assessors have to monitor not only the performance of candidates in terms of manner and frequency of contribution but also the content – checking for factual errors as well as assessing the impact of ideas on the group. All agree that Gordon was good when he spoke, but he didn't speak enough and that Martin and Alan were fairly ineffectual. There is animated discussion over John – was he too forthright, bossy even – and Richard, were his contributions always as well formulated as they should be? Eventually marks are arrived at.

Lunch with the panel at the cafe in the local church crypt is enjoyable; the conversation interesting and wide-ranging. Back at 2pm and while the candidates do the in-tray and letter-writing exercises, the panel go over the policy exercise. Gordon has done exceptionally well.

At 4pm I sit in on the psychologist's interview with Alan. His answers are wandering, though at times (intentionally) amusing. He has an innocence about him. Afterwards, Dennis said it had been like interviewing a sixteen year old.

At the end of each interview the panel come together to report back. Although marks are not given, the feedback allows for more sharing of information and each can alert the others to issues or aspects of character that might usefully be explored further.

At 5pm I join Susan for Richard's interview. Yet again, he does not always express his ideas as clearly as would be expected from someone of his excellent academic background. Even his arguments on the topics he had suggested are a bit wobbly. Susan argues back hard and at one point actually tells him to '...come on, come back at me.' Susan's conclusion is that Richard doesn't yet have the self-confidence to stand by his convictions and make decisions easily; always he wants to have more information.

The feedback and general discussion goes on until 6.30, long after the candidates have left for a well-deserved dinner and evening of relaxation.

Day 2: *For the applicants, the day starts with preparation for the second group exercise. In this one, each candidate is given information on one of eight topics which follow on from the issue in the policy exercise. They study this for 30 minutes before the session. During the exercise they will have to chair the discussion. Their colleagues will only have had 3 minutes to read the topic brief during the exercise itself, so it is important that the Chair of each subject starts by summarising the main points clearly and suggesting preferred solutions. Each candidate has 15 minutes on his topic.*

Again the assessors scribble notes like mad, on content and presentation as well as performance as Chair and group member. Richard is reasonably good in the chair though, again, shows some lack of decisiveness. Alan and Martin do not perform well. Indeed Martin's introduction, though detailed, is actually misleading and a confused discussion ensues. Alan just has no presence, or as the panel later agreed, no 'oomph factor'. John is very brisk and businesslike and does bring everyone into the discussion, though at a pace that Michael finds problematic. Gordon comes up trumps. His introduction is succinct, his suggested options are sound and he chairs the discussion well. His summing up is of an appropriate length and accurate.

Marks are given separately for chairing and as a group member. All agree that Gordon performed very well and that Alan and Martin did not. Once again, most discussion was over Richard's mixed performance and John's possible tendency to dominate.

While the panel had been talking over the second group exercise, the candidates had done another written exercise. These papers, plus the letters previously completed, have now come through. Over a sandwich lunch, the letters and technical summaries are shuffled round amongst the panel in their various rooms — as Susan rightly says 'like a French farce'. There is pretty much a consensus on mark for these. Gordon is now appearing as the front-runner and John, who seems so confident, has some question marks hanging over his judgment.

In the afternoon I sit in on two interviews with Michael – those with Gordon and John. As the Chair of the Panel, Michael is the only one to have read and marked the in-tray exercise, so at least half the interviews are taken up with its discussion. He also likes to give them a business oriented question, e.g. you've inherited a failing business, how will you turn it around? Thereafter, some time is left for a general discussion of one of the candidate's chosen topics and / or one of Michael's choosing.

Gordon performs well on the in-tray element and adequately on the business questions, if a bit slow on the uptake. He looks tired now. Reasonable on his own subject, he plods rather than sparkles on Michael's question about the validity of peacekeeping operations.

Last session of the day is John's interview. On the in-tray, he seems to be trying to suss out the answer Michael wants rather than saying what he really thinks. The bombshell, though, is on his own topic. He holds some pretty controversial views on euthanasia. As purely personal beliefs they would not be a problem, but when Michael challenges on the social and political acceptability of action based on his views, he really doesn't seem to see any problem. Just as surprising as his lack of political nous, is his failure to pick up on the effect his answer was having on Michael, who is obviously taken aback by John's inability to recognise the political implications of his ideas.

At around 5pm with their ordeal finally over, the candidates leave for home. The panel re-convenes. Susan reports (to the pleasant surprise of all) that Martin had done well in his interview and was actually very interesting to talk to. Nothing much new on the others. The real surprise, of course, was John.

Day 3: *The morning of day three is when the marks are finally agreed and the recommendations made. Each candidate is looked at again in his entirety. The panel member leading summarises the application form once more and then each element over the two days is reviewed and marks finalised.*

Individual marks are given for specific skills, then an overall CSSB mark is arrived at. 1, 2 and 3 are passes, 4 is a near miss and 5, 6 and 7 are definite fails.

Richard provokes a long discussion, almost an hour. Should he be a 4 or a 5? The panel decides on a 5 but with the recommendation that he should get some experience (and confidence) outside academia and re-apply in 1-3 years. Alan and Martin will no doubt find their niches, but it is not to be in the fast stream. Both are deemed definite 6s. Apart from his performance in the first group exercise and a slightly lacklustre interview with Michael at the end, Gordon has done very well. All agree he is a pass, though they debate whether he should be a 2 or a 3. John is also discussed at some length, but with puzzlement more than anything else. There is no doubt that he is a fail. Obviously able in many ways, his personal style was not appropriate and his apparent lack of political judgment was the nail in his coffin.

At 12.30 I say goodbye leaving the panel members to spend the afternoon writing up the mountain of paperwork.

And if you succeed?: Hopefully, you will get offered a post in your first choice option; though this isn't guaranteed. If you pass, you will definitely be made a job offer, but you may need to settle for your second or third option. Successful CSSB graduates who want the Diplomatic Service or Clerks Department will have to go through one more stage (probably an interview) before being offered a place on those schemes.

Financially, the rewards are about average for graduate recruitment. Starting salaries will vary between departments and according to experience and qualifications. The salary range for the three to four years on the Fast Stream programme is currently £19,000–£33,000 and most people will start around the bottom of the scale. Subsequent pay increases are linked to your level of responsibility and individual performance. On promotion out of the fast stream programme (usually within 3-4 years), the immediate salary range goes up to around £48,000.

For those who do not succeed: If you don't make it on to the fast stream programme first time round, you can always try again. You can re-take the Qualifying Tests and if you got through to CSSB, you will get feed back on your performance there. This will help you identify areas for development and may help you choose the best route to gain relevant expertise and experience.

A recent innovation is the offer of a mainstream post for those who narrowly fail CSSB. In fact, you may decide that mainstream entry is more appropriate or attractive anyway. Plus, once you're in, some departments will nominate suitable mainstreamers for the fast stream and you won't have to go through the Qualifying Test.

Summary   **General Fast Stream**

Requirements:	*Education*: Minimum 2.2 degree in any subject. 'A' level European Language (or equivalent ability) for European Fast Stream
	Nationality: UK National, and for Diplomatic Service, British Citizen
	Age limit: 41 for European Fast Stream, none for other options
	Equal Opportunities: Applications welcomed from all
	Relevant Work Experience: Useful, but not required
	Relevant Postgrad. Qual: Useful, but not required
Selection Procedure:	• Application form from Capita RAS
	• Two closing dates: September and January (For Diplomatic Service must apply in September)
	• Aptitude and biodata tests (with exemptions available for those with a disability)
	• 2-day assessment centre
	• Final selection procedure for Diplomatic Service and Clerks (probably interview and day spent in Service/Department)
Key Skills and Qualities	• People skills (interpersonal sensitivity and persuasiveness); task skills (problem solving, innovation); personal skills (drive, resilience, adaptability).
Geographical availability	• The majority of Home Civil Service fast stream posts are in London, with some opportunities in Scotland, Wales and Northern Ireland.
	• In Diplomatic Service first overseas posting is usually within two to three years
Pay and Conditions	*Starting pay scales*: £19,000–£33,000 depending on qualifications and experience. On promotion from fast stream, pay band up to £48,000. Thereafter in pay bands up to top of range for Permanent Secretary of approx. £170,000.
	Promotion: on merit.
	• Probationary period of 1-2 years (time varies between departments)

> *Holidays:*Vary between departments, but from 22-25 days plus 10.5 days public and other discretionary days
>
> *Job Security:*Very good
>
> • Limit on degree of party political activity allowed

Further Information

- Fast Stream
  Capita RAS
  Innovation Court
  New Street, Basingstoke
  Hampshire RG21 7JB
  Tel: 01256 383 683
  www.faststream.gov.uk
- The Cabinet Office website (Civil Service page) has excellent information on recruitment and links to sites for more information including sandwich placements, vacation employment, and opportunities by degree discipline.
  www.cabinet-office.gov.uk
- Or go straight to the Fast Stream page via
- To get links to any Civil Service department (and many other organisations) go to the Open Government site and click on Organisation Index
  www.open.gov.uk
- The FCO offers briefings on careers on the last Friday each month. For information on this and on Diplomatic Service Overseas Attachments for undergraduates and work experience in London for 16–17 year olds, go to the Foreign and Commonwealth Office (FCO) site
  www.fco.gov.uk
- For information on the other Fast Stream schemes not covered in the chapter, contact:

  Economists
  Economic Management Group Unit
  HM Treasury Parliament Street
  London SW1P 3AG
  Tel: 020 7270 5073

www.ges.gov.uk

Statisticians
GSS Personnel
Office for National Statistics
Zone D4/22
1 Drummond Gate
London SW1V 2QQ
Tel: 020 7533 5040/5043
www.statistics.gov.uk

Government Communications Headquarters (GCHQ)
Room A/1108, GCHQ
Prior Road
Cheltenham GL52 5AJ
Tel: 01242 232912
www.gchq.gov.uk

Inland Revenue
Human Resources Division
Mowbray House
PO Box 55
Castle Meadow Road
Nottingham NG2 1BE
Tel: 0115 9740603
www.inlandrevenue.gov.uk

Selected Reading

- *Civil Service Yearbook* (The Stationery Office. Annual publication, also on CD Rom). This is a mine of information: Civil Service employment statistics, details of departments and their personnel, and much more.
- *The Diplomatic Service List..* (The Stationery Office. Annual publication). Lists all Foreign and Commonwealth Office departments in UK, with contact names. Addresses of all British Representatives Overseas. Biographical list of staff.
- *How to Be A Civil Servant*, Martin Stanley (Politico's Publishing)
- *How to Pass the Civil Service Qualifying Exams*, Mike Bryon. London: Kogan Page

5   Civil Service main stream

The variety of jobs in the Main Stream is enormous. Many will be for specific professions, vets, surveyors, etc., but others are appropriate for those with arts and social science backgrounds and an interest in politics and/or social policy. The four areas covered here (Operational Entry in the Diplomatic Service, Executive Officer in the Cabinet Office, Research Analyst in the Foreign Office and Research staff in the Home Office) cover both practical, hands-on roles as well as two very different kinds of research. The people profiled come from a variety of backgrounds, are different ages and at varying stages in their careers to give you an indication of the range of people employed in the Civil Service

Main Stream jobs are advertised in a number of places. Departments are responsible for their own recruitment and each may use different sources. Many will use Capita Ras (employment agency) and increasingly, their own websites. They may also advertise nationally or just in the local press. If in doubt, phone the departments you are interested in and ask for details. Do not send in your CV on a speculative basis. Strict adherence to the rules of open and fair competition means that all departments will advertise their vacancies.

The Diplomatic Service – operational entry

There are three points of entry into the Diplomatic Service depending on qualifications and the type of work. The lowest is Executive Assistant; up one is Operational Entry which requires a minimum of GCSEs plus substantial work experience, or a degree; and up again is Policy Entrant, i.e. Fast Stream. Eleanor Petch's diary in the Fast Stream chapter will have given you some idea of the type of work undertaken by a new(ish) Policy Entrant to the Diplomatic Service. Operational Grade staff on the other hand, are concerned much more with the practical side of the Service's work. This doesn't rule out all policy work, some postings will certainly involve this, particularly as you gain experience and move up the promotion pathway. However, for the most part Operational Grades do help 'to make things happen', as the recruitment literature says. You could be organising recruitment in London or helping British nationals who have got into trouble or fallen on hard times abroad or dealing with a hundred and one other situations in the UK and worldwide which require intelligence and patience and, most of all, common sense and a practical approach.

After an initial maximum of three years in London, about two thirds of your postings will be abroad. You will have a certain amount of say in where you go. Every 6 weeks or so, a list of opportunities is published for which staff who are coming to the end of their current posting can bid, i.e. apply. For overseas opportunities, you can choose 12, in order of preference. Obviously not all opportunities are equally appealing and included in this list must be two 'hardship' posts. A whole range of factors is taken into account when deciding which posts are 'difficult'; it could be poor sanitation or housing, security issues or, for women, working in a country where the religion or culture limits their personal freedom. When you make your 12 selections, you have to be as prepared to go to your twelfth as your first. Which posting you will get is determined by a board of selectors who look at your personal file – previous experience, marks for appraisals, reports on assessment centres etc. – there is no interview.

One career: Colin Duncan is 12 years into his career with the Diplomatic Service. He was educated in Scotland and after his highers (A level equivalent) and a year on a business studies course he was lured to apply for an Executive Assistant level post by the variety of the work and the opportunity to travel. He spent three years in London, first in the Financial Policy Department doing basic administrative work (dealing with expense claims and so on) and then working in a Minister's private office making travel arrangements, keeping the diary and generally liaising with the private secretary.

Colin was then posted to Brussels where he spent the next two and a half years doing a very different kind of work, as he explains: 'This was a political job. I was going to Plenary Meetings of the Council of Europe in Strasbourg and Luxembourg and reporting back to London. I was also working at the European Parliament in Brussels and feeding back developments there into the system in London. Another part of the job was assisting the Press Officer with regard to UK policy, lines to take, defending our position and liaising with the media and organising press meetings.'

Promotion to the Operational Grade followed and prior to a three-year posting in Bulgaria, he returned to London for relevant training. 'I was in London for just a couple of months and took a 3-week course in embassy management which covered how an embassy operates, how to manage the staff and the resources and so on. This was followed by a consular course because, although it wasn't going to be my job on a day-to-day basis, I would be standing in for the Vice- Consul – that's the person who looks after British nationals in trouble.'

After his stint in Bulgaria, Colin spent a year and a half on 'floating duties'. As it sounds, this is where you 'float', i.e. move from post to post, wherever you are needed to cover for holidays, sickness etc. There are only about 20 positions of this sort and they are always at operational level or below. In the 18 months, Colin worked in 13 countries around the world, and each for just 3 weeks to a couple of months. How hard was this? 'Well, you've certainly got to be flexible, resilient and adaptable. Not only was I adjusting to new countries but also each time I moved I was doing an entirely different job. I could be Deputy Head of the Mission in a small post like Phnom Penh in Cambodia but the following week find myself in Amsterdam as Vice-Consul. You not only go from one end of the world to the other at the weekend, but have to start work on Monday morning in a different job, different people, different culture and, sometimes, under arduous circumstances.'

Now back in London, Colin is working in the Recruitment Section and has had another promotion. He successfully completed a two-day Assessment and Development Centre which involved a series of role plays, interviews and tests for the required competencies, i.e. skills. He is now in what is called Band C, which equates to policy entrant and he may indeed be competing against policy officers for overseas postings, though this won't be until 2003 when his current stint in the UK is over. Because many of the embassies now have less than 5 UK based staff, far fewer than in previous times, you do not have to be as senior to become an ambassador. So is there anything to stop Colin setting his sights on that? 'No, nothing. We're moving away from the old, 'you can only be an ambassador if you've been to Oxbridge'. We look for the best people for the job. If you can pass the assessment centres you can compete with everyone. Obviously it's taken me much longer to progress, but the possibilities are there.' In fact, you can sit the assessment centre to go into Band C when you have been in the operational grade (Band B) for 5 years, or slightly sooner if your line manager recommends you.

Recruitment and Selection: Recruitment to the Operational Point Entry takes place annually with a closing date in January. Although a degree is not required, many applicants these days are graduates, but as well as your qualifications you must be able to prove that you possess the relevant competencies, and are able to withstand the rigours of overseas life. Competition is fierce. In 2001 there were 1924 applications for 70 places. A full statistical breakdown is available for 2000 and shows that of the successful applicants 80% were graduates and 20% joined after A levels. The average age was 29 (although the oldest successful candidate was 40), 48% were women and 2 were from ethnic minorities.

The selection procedure consists of four elements.

1   The initial application form which is just checked for compliance with age, nationality and GCSE English and Maths required.

2   Verbal and numerical reasoning aptitude tests of half an hour each.

3   A written test where you are required to produce 4 pieces of work; for example a draft letter or telegram based on information you will have been given.

4   An interview with a panel of 3 selectors.

Any job offer then made is subject to security vetting which takes about 4 months and from application to starting in post takes almost a year.

Summary   **Diplomatic Service – Operational Point Entry**

Requirements

Education: 5 GCSEs including English and Maths plus 5 year's work experience or 2 A levels (and GCSEs as above) plus 3 year's work experience or a degree and adequate demonstration of the required competencies

Nationality: British and have been a British citizen for at least 5 years prior to applications and have been resident in the UK for the 5 years preceding application

Age limit: 52

Equal Opportunities: Applications welcome from all

Relevant Work Experience: Work experience that demonstrates relevant skills is required for those with qualifications below degree level and advantageous for graduates

Relevant Postgrad. Qual: No

Selection Procedure

• Application form (from Centre Point Group, see Further Information at the end of this chapter for address); verbal and numerical aptitude tests, written test; panel interview

Key Skills and Qualities

• You will be assessed against 14 competencies: initiative and responsibility; adaptability and creativity; resilience; analysis and judgement; expertise and specialist skills; relating to others; teamwork; contacts and representation; influence; managing people; managing operations and resources; service delivery; written and oral communication.

Pay and Conditions

Starting salaries: £16,576 – £18,576 rising to £24,205

Promotion: to Band C on successful completion of assessment centre.

Salary scale £18,741-£29,732

Holidays: 25 days rising to 30 after 12 years, plus public holidays

Job security: Very Good

• Limit on degree of political activity allowed

Cabinet office – graduate recruitment

Traditionally all Executive Officer level posts in the Civil Service required a minimum of 2 A levels. However in recent years individual departments have been able to stipulate their own selection criteria and the Cabinet Office operates its B1 recruitment scheme for Executive Officers which is open only to graduates.

The Cabinet Office works closely with all the Civil Service Departments as well as No. 10 and is involved in co-ordinating government as well as helping to bring about organisational reform within the Civil Service itself. Given the broad remit of the Cabinet Office, the roles for B1 staff are obviously many and varied, but one example to give you a flavour of the work is that of Helen Gee. She graduated in History and Geography from Roehampton Institute of Higher Education in 1997 and initially worked as an administrative officer in Customs and Excise. 'I kind of fell into the Civil Service by accident. I just needed a job straight after university.' In Customs, Helen gained experience in administration and organisation but was attracted to the Cabinet Office not only because it meant promotion but also precisely because it does have an overview of the whole Civil Service.

In her first eighteen months Helen worked in the Change Management Division which, as its name suggests, is responsible for co-ordinating a programme of change across all Civil Service Departments. She describes the range of tasks she was involved in:

✓ *Some research projects. I'd provide my managers with summaries of reports on change management and better deals for staff.*

✓ *Day-to-day management of finance – ensuring that all records reconciled, profiling expenditure for each month, identifying and resolving any problems, providing management information on financial status and contributing to the annual divisional bids for funding.*

✓ *Running 4 regional conferences for a total of 1000 civil servants. Research and selecting the venues, managing the event organisers' contract, contributing to the design of the programme and helping out on the day.*

✓ *Communications work – promoting and informing staff about the change programme, for example, designing the Civil Service reform*

> *website, putting together a monthly newsletter and running workshops for the Internal Communicators Network.*

✓ *Management, and supporting the development, of one administrative officer.*

Within the Civil Service staff do change roles quite frequently (which for many people is one of the attractions of the work) and the Cabinet Office is no exception. In April 2001 Helen moved to the Learning Strategy Division as a policy adviser on management development programmes and assessment centres. She continues to have responsibility for one member of staff and the day-to-day management of finance, but is now also involved in creating policy on 'talent spotting'. This, as she explains is where the Service 'identifies talented people and develops them. We give them varied experiences so that they reach their full potential. The idea is that this takes place at all levels, but preferably we want to catch people early on. It is part of the 'bringing on talent initiative' of the Civil Service Reform programme.' This aspect of the job involves Helen in 'advising and guiding departments on their work on talent spotting management and assessment centres through running workshops, monitoring what departments are doing and sharing good practice from the public and private sectors.'

So, you can see that the work involves a whole range of tasks including organisation, human resource management, policy development, financial management and training. Such a job demands the development of an equally wide range of skills which is why the selection process stresses practical competencies and your ability to deliver.

Selection: The minimum educational requirement is a lower second class degree in any subject, but the initial application form also asks for specific information about what you have done, how you approached tasks and what the outcomes were. As Helen remembers it 'there were 4 key questions which looked at things like delivery of results, communication skills and leading a project – each with a 100 word limit.' Competition is fierce – In September 2000 around 1000 people applied for the 20 vacancies, so the application form has to be good to stand out. The vast majority of successful candidates were new graduates, but, like Helen, 20-25% had previously worked in other jobs either in, or outside, the Civil Service and could draw on that experience for their forms.

Those who were shortlisted went to a formal panel interview of 3 people which continued the theme of practicalities and, says Helen, 'focused on previous experiences and how you would carry out tasks, such as creating new policy. But you also needed to be aware of current affairs particularly those affecting the Cabinet Office, for example the Modernising Government programme.' You can read up on the modernising and reforming of the Civil Service on the Cabinet Office website.

The Rewards: A little wistfully Helen says, 'I sometimes wish the money was a bit better [starting scale is £15,836 – £20,931] but there is a non-contributory pension and the leave in combination with the privilege days off are good [25 days annual leave plus 8 Bank Holidays and 2.5 privilege days]. I am partially deaf and rely on hearing aids and lip-reading to communicate and I've found the Civil Service very positive about my disability. There is a Disability in the Cabinet Office network which is a support group set up and run by disabled staff. We are consulted by teams working on personnel policies to ensure that disability needs are covered, and are working to increase colleagues' awareness of disabilities.'

Summary   **Executive Officer (B1) – Cabinet Office**

Role	• Varied. To facilitate the work of the Cabinet Office and/or particular units within it.
Requirements	*Education*: Degree in any discipline (min. 2.2)
	Nationality: None specified
	Age limit: None specified
	Equal Opportunities: Applications welcome from all
	Relevant work experience: Can be useful but not essential
	Relevant postgrad. qual.: None required
Selection Procedure	• Vacancies advertised via Capita Ras (see Further Information) and in the *Guardian*,

	• The *Evening Standard* and possibly others such as the *Voice*
	• Application form and panel interview
Key Skills and Qualities	• Leadership and management of people; delivery of results, prioritising, communication, personal effectiveness
Pay and Conditions	*Starting scale*: £15,836 – £20,931
	Hours: Normal office hours
	Holidays 25 days annual leave plus 10.5 Bank Holidays and privilege days
	Probation: One year
	Promotion: Based on performance and vacancies being available to Higher Executive Officer (B2) £20,600 – £31,519 then to Band A £32,000 – £48,329
	Job Security:Very good
	Some limit on political activities

Research Analysts, Foreign and Commonwealth Office (FCO)

Within the FCO and the Diplomatic Service there are obviously many people with extensive knowledge of international affairs. However, Research Analysts are a distinct group of experts whose primary role is to provide information, analysis and advice to members of FCO staff and other Whitehall Departments.

There are approximately 60 Research Analysts (even numbers of men and women) working in 9 groups. Eight of these are concerned with specific areas of the world and the 9th, The Global Issues Research Group, deals with international institutions, human rights, the environment etc. Janet Gunn is Head of the 12-strong Eastern Research Group which covers the area of the former Soviet Union: 'We maintain a broad range of expertise; we're expected to be political scientist, economist and historian all rolled into one. We have to a keep a broad view of what's happening in our areas so in that sense we do not do research in the same way as university academics. About 50% of our work is responding to requests for comments, analysis or background information, often to very tight deadlines. Most of our work is short and snappy – a few pages long – and we give oral briefings or take part in departmental discussions. But we also work on our own initiative. When we spot something of relevance we will write a note on it.'

To write a 'short and snappy' note on a complex subject is a real talent and the description belies the extensive knowledge that underpins such a briefing. Research Analysts must be constantly updating their knowledge and expanding their understanding and part of that process involves attending seminars and conferences, many of which are organised by the Research Analysts themselves. The Eastern Group arranges a seminar approximately every six weeks and the total number organised by all the research groups could be up to 40 or 50 a year. As Janet Gunn explains, 'their purpose is to inform the policy-making process. They are not open to the public or written up for public consumption but they do provide a very important bridge with the academic world and outside expertise in general.' During their careers Research Analysts are also able to publish papers and books on their topics, but these usually have to be written in their own time and have to be submitted for screening before being sent to a publisher.

The majority of Research Analysts are permanent members of staff, but some (usually known as Research Fellows) are on fixed-term contracts of one to three years. All Analysts are encouraged to visit their areas, and are able to bid for full-length postings overseas. There is no pressure to spend a specific amount of time broad, and in the 30 years that Janet Gunn has been at the FCO she has undertaken two full postings abroad (about 3 years each) and two shorter attachments of a few months. Research Analysts abroad would continue to do political analysis but would also become involved in the whole range of an embassy's work.

Selection and Promotion: Vacancies occur reasonably frequently. They are advertised on the Capita RAS website and in specialist journals relevant to the areas. Older members of staff may have joined after their first degree but these days a masters or PhD relevant to the post is a must. Fluency in a relevant language is specified by some research groups, otherwise, an aptitude for learning languages is certainly required.

Selection is by application form followed by a one-day assessment centre. This usually involves two exercises similar to those used by the general fast stream; namely an individual policy exercise and a group discussion to arrive at recommendations. It is unlikely that either of these exercises will relate directly to your area of expertise or even to international affairs in general. They are used to test your analytical, teamwork and communication skills in general. (For more information please refer to the Chapter on Fast Stream selection.) There will also be an interview of up to one hour with a panel of selectors including one or two Research Analysts and an outside expert on the subject area.

Promotion is through five grades from research officer to research counsellor. Heads of Research Groups can be on any of the top three grades/salaries, though the majority of their work will always be research with management taking just 20-30% of their time. As Janet Gunn says: 'Promotion prospects overall are not far reaching, but for those with a real interest in international affairs in general and their specific countries in particular, job satisfaction is very high.'

Summary   **Research Analysts**

Role	To provide specialist information, analysis and advice to FCO staff and other Whitehall departments.
Requirements	*Relevant postgraduate degree*: masters or doctorate
	Nationality: British citizen with a close connection to the UK
	Security vetting: Yes
	Equal Opportunities: Applications welcome from all
Selection Procedure	• Application form from Capita RAS (see Further Information); one-day assessment centre including an individual and group exercises plus a panel interview
Key Skills and Qualities	• Sound knowledge of the area; research/analytical skills; judgement; communication skills
Pay and Conditions	*Salary*: £17,468–£35,449
	• There is a limit on the degree of political activity allowed

Research staff – The Home Office

In order to devise appropriate policies and monitor their effectiveness, the government requires detailed and in-depth information on just about all areas of life affected by domestic policy. The main home Civil Service departments each have their sections devoted to compiling such information and in the Home Office it is called the Research Development and Statistics Directorate (RDS). Over 300 members of staff – researchers, statisticians, economists and operational researchers – beaver away covering the subjects of responsibility of the Home Office. The largest area is obviously to do with policing and criminal justice, but also important is the Immigration and Community Unit which covers areas such as Citizenship, Immigration and Asylum, Race Relations and Voluntary and Community Research. The Head of the latter section is Meta Zimmeck,

An American by birth, Meta first came to England to do some research into the history of employment of women in the British Civil Service for her American PhD thesis. Little did she know then that many years on, at the age of 52, she would become a civil servant herself. But between then and April 2000 when she became a Principal Research Officer she was, as she says, 'a jobbing researcher. I'd been asked to do work, I'd applied for work, I'd generated work and set up projects and funding. I'd never been out of work. Basically I was a researcher for hire.' Though a historian by academic training, and with experience of archival work at the Public Record Office, she gradually moved across into social research. 'I got interested in housing because I was a tenant of a housing association, so I shifted over to housing research. Then, because housing associations are voluntary organisations, I started doing bits and pieces on the voluntary sector. Then I worked with the Royal Society of Arts (RSA) on the 'Redefining Work' project and got very excited about voluntary sector employment. In a way there's a kind of pattern to my background, but it's rather obscure.' Obscure it may be, but definitely relevant to the work of the Voluntary and Community unit.

Initially, Meta's work at the RDS was just another 'jobbing researcher' post because it was a temporary 4-month contract, but when the permanent job as head of the section came up, she went for it. Her team comprises of two Senior Research Officers and two student trainees. The Home Office has a long tradition of offering students from a variety of disciplines 12-month sandwich placements. The current students, one studying Sociology the other Management, are full members of the team and take responsibility for specific projects as Meta explains. 'One of them has volunteering in prisons which she's basically managed. I wrote the questionnaire and did the high level negotiation to get the show on the road, but she set up the coding frames, designed secondary questionnaires and is now doing the data analysis. I just keep a watching brief and give her whatever support she needs. The other student is doing befriending and mentoring. Because we've had to farm out some of this she's had a bit more of a managerial role in the sense of having to do the day to day management with the research company.' Some of the research is done in-house, but because many of the projects involve huge numbers of questionnaires and high volumes of data analysis, much of it is contracted out to market or other types of research companies, voluntary organisations, academics etc., whoever is appropriate. The largest piece of work at the moment is the Citizenship Survey which, amongst other things, looks at social capital issues and different types of voluntary and community activities – from helping a neighbour to writing a letter to an MP to leading a group or organisation. This is being done jointly by a number of sections in the Home Office and includes a 15,000-person survey to be done every two years.

Even when work is contracted out the initial planning is done by Meta and her team and the overall management responsibility and monitoring remains with team members involved. The final report is often Meta's work, though the students may have contributed drafts and throughout their year in the section 'they certainly pull their weight'.

Placements: Placements for penultimate year undergraduates are advertised on the RDS website and also in the 'Civil Service Sandwich Course Placements' booklet available in university careers service. The closing date for applications varies slightly from year to year but it may be as early as December so do keep an eye out. Applicants should be studying relevant subjects such as social science or numerate subjects and selection is by written application and interview, plus an Open

Day for the allocation of placements to successful applicants. The salary in 2001 was £12,160 and the holiday allowance was 22 days.

Other Roles: Meta Zimmeck is not alone in taking up a senior post in the RDS later on in her working life, her immediate line manager had previously worked in advertising and market research. However, many people will join the permanent staff at the entry point of Research Officer where you will play your part in designing and carrying out major research programmes. To find out more about the type of research undertaken by the RDS and see samples of their work visit the website at www.homeoffice.gov.uk/rds. Research Officers require a relevant degree, such as social science, criminology, maths or economics and, again, vacancies are advertised on the RDS website. Application is by form, interview and usually an exercise to test analytical skills. The starting salary range is £17,134–£24,477 plus a £1,903 recruitment and retention allowance.

An Outsider's View: People coming to one organisation with experience of others often provide valuable insights about the culture, the strengths and weaknesses. Having been self-employed for many years, was it hard for Meta to settle in to her first 'proper job' in a bureaucracy? ' Having to consult people on just about everything, though it can stop you making truly terrible mistakes, it can also stop you doing anything at all. And, there is a very formal system of written performance appraisal which I really hated at first, but when I went through it with someone I realised that for all it's faults it's a unique chance to look at any misunderstandings and other issues. But I've been very impressed with how hard working people are and how dedicated. There is a strong emphasis on training and I've been pleasantly surprised by how non-standard the Civil Service has become. Certainly the pre-1939 Civil Service I knew in London as a historian was entirely rigid – people never changed department and they rarely changed grade – it's so different now.'

Summary   **Research Officer**

| *Role* | • Social research. To gather, analyse and interpret information on the areas covered by the Home Office in order to inform policy decision-making. |

Requirements	*Education:* Usually upper second class degree in a social science or numerate subject
	Nationality: None specified
	Age limit: None specified
	Equal Opportunities: Applications open to all
	Relevant work experience: Not required
	Relevant postgraduate: Not required
Selection Procedure	• Jobs advertised on RDS website and Capita Ras website
	• Application by form, interview and test of analytical skills
Key Skills and Qualities	• Numeracy and ability to manipulate statistical data. Good presentation skills, report-writing, organisational ability, time management and teamwork.
Pay and Conditions	*Starting salary:* £17,134 – £24,477 plus £1,903 Recruitment and Retention (R&R) allowance
	Hours: Normal office hours
	Holidays: 22 days plus Bank Holidays
	Probation: 1 year
	Promotion: Based on performance and vacancies being available to Senior Research Officer (£24,371 – £34,186 plus (£1,903 R&R allowance). Then to Principal Research Officer (£33,344 – £47,634 + R&R).

Further information

• The Diplomatic Service Operational Entry vacancies are handled by Centre Point Group at 16 St Helen's Place, London EC3A 6DP. Tel: 020 7562 1690, www.centrepointgroup.co.uk

• The Foreign and Commonwealth Office (FCO) holds careers briefing sessions on the last Friday in each month. Their Overseas Undergraduate Attachment Scheme is open to those seriously considering a career as a policy or operational entrant in the Diplomatic Service. And, the FCO also operates a work experience scheme for 16–17 year-olds when you would spend

2 weeks at the FCO in London. See the website for more information and contact details www.fco.gov.uk

Other Departments' vacancies are often handled by Capita Ras and advertised on their website at www.rasnet.co.uk. Their address is Innovation Court, New Street, Basingstoke, Hants RG21 7JB

- Many Departmental websites carry vacancies and possibly general careers information including profiles of current staff/role. Links to all Civil Service Departments (and many other organisations) from www.open.gov.uk

Interview   **Mike O'Connor CBE**

Mike O'Connor is the Director of the Millennium Commission. You might well have seen him being interviewed on television whenever the issue of grants to the Millennium Dome came up. He started his career as a Civil Service Fast Streamer and subsequently worked in pressure groups and as a self-employed consultant

CV

Education

BSc (Hons) Physics and Geology, Keele University

MSc Social & Economic Aspects of Science & Technology, Imperial College, London

Career

1982–9 Civil Service

1989–92 Director of the Coronary Prevention Group

1992–3 Consultant in Public Health Policy

1993–6 Director for Developed Economies at Consumers International

1996–8 Director of Policy and Corporate Affairs at the Millennium Commission

1998– Director of the Millennium Commission

Was it at Keele that you became interested in politics?

No, I'd always been interested in politics. I think it was my childhood. I was brought up in Ireland and in quite a strong Catholic background. As I grew up, I became less religious but the concern I had about matters of right and wrong, which were initially ones of faith and religion, became issues of politics. When I went to Keele and started to mix with people who were studying politics, economics and philosophy etc., I got more interested in politics and less and less interested in science. So I then went on to a postgraduate degree which was more related to political issues.

Were you politically active at university?

I couldn't really get involved in student politics, but that reflects the rest of my life, I've never been able to get to grips with representative politics anyway. I'm not a politician. I was much more interested in the study, the theoretical and the abstract than in standing up and saying ' vote for me, bring me your babies to kiss'. I was never at ease with standing for office and fighting on some of the issues that were around at the time.

You have said elsewhere, that you made 200 job applications at the beginning of the 80s. What sort of jobs were you going for?

I wanted to work for a trade union as a research officer. I got as far as one interview and lost out to Peter Hain [now a Government minister]. *My lack of a background in formal political jobs didn't make it easy. I was this university lad and I was competing against some very good people, like Peter Hain. But I applied to lots of other jobs as well. I remember I applied for a job as a patent agent and the person who interviewed me said I had had the education of the second son of an earl, I'd dabbled in science and social science. I know now when I'm reviewing CVs, you tend to pick out the people who are archetypally suited to your particular job. Somebody who looks a bit odd, degree here degree there, you don't always take the time you should to look at those people. So I think I was a victim of that. I only got the job in the Civil Service because they tested allcomers.*

In the 1980s, Oxbridge entrants still dominated the Civil Service. Did you find it difficult to fit in?

Well the biggest problem for me frankly wasn't about Oxbridge and non-Oxbridge, it was the apartheid system whereby people like me entered with a gold star round our neck and other graduates, people my age, were kept separate [executive officer level]. That was like an elite club. I didn't have a problem with the Oxbridge people, although to be fair I was in the Department of Health and Social Security where that was less prevalent I think. Other departments might have been more difficult, but no, I very much enjoyed the Civil Service.

It was a nice environment because it was very meritocratic, and it wasn't too competitive; people weren't trying to edge each other out all the time. Since I've left, I've worked in environments with much more people manoeuvring and personal politics. The Civil Service is interesting in that although it works in a political arena, the personal politics are much less marked. All the politics is shoved upstairs to the ministers or perhaps to the most senior officials.

Were you at the DHSS the whole time?

No, I went on secondment to a joint unit of Cabinet Office and Treasury. That was interesting because the culture was quite different and, I have to say, was more stimulating. People there seemed to have more freedom to challenge and innovate. And they were more open to the outside, with the press for example.

You said in an article that one of the reasons you wanted to leave the Civil Service was the lack of freedom to innovate. If you'd have been moved to a different department permanently do you think you would have stayed?

I don't think so. I couldn't see the rest of my life in the velvet drainpipe – comfortable but constricting. I left because all the prizes were for not getting something wrong. That may have been different in other departments, but I think at that time in my life my desire to go out and change things was so strong I could not have been kept there. This was in 1989 when the prospect of any political change was remote. Colleagues I left behind in the Civil Service said that the change of government in 1997 was a breath of fresh air. Whatever their political views, to have a change of government, just somebody new to come and shake things up a bit, that is a great opportunity for civil servants. If you are just ploughing the same road year after year, a new government coming in is a chance to innovate and change things.

You were at Coronary Prevention Group (CPG) for a fairly short amount of time?

Almost everything in my career has been for a relatively short time. In the Civil Service you move on quite quickly, and I like that. So for me, doing two or three years is really quite a long time. CPG was a campaigning organisation which appealed to me because I actually wanted to go out and have some formative influence on policy. My career has always been one of trying to choose between being within the establishment and having quite a lot of power but not much freedom, or on the other hand being outside and having lots of freedom but very little power. For me going to CPG was a leap to the freedom with no power.

Did you feel at the end of your time there that you had achieved much?

Yes. I saw us as a noisy pressure group. Given the size of the organisation and the resources, we made a hell of a lot of noise. We got an immense amount of coverage and the issues on which we fought, such as tobacco advertising and food labelling, have paid off. I think I brought a lot to that because of my knowledge of the tobacco industry from the DHSS.

I certainly learned a lot personally. Coming from the Civil Service, I was completely unaware of many political issues about people management and managing boards. I suppose, I was quite naive. It was the first time I had ever been exposed to the media and I think that I did well. I also think we achieved quite a lot for the people who worked in the organisation. People grew in CPG and went on to great things.

Developing people is something I take pride in. That is an achievement as well.

Then you left CPG to become self-employed as a consultant. Why?

One of the things that worried me about the voluntary sector was that I didn't think we were terribly good at campaigning; we were too fragmented, too many of us, small organisations, never reaching critical mass. Therefore the battles we were fighting we weren't winning because we weren't coming together and focussing and strategising well enough. The idea of alliances appealed to me very much. I knew of an organisation in America called the Advocacy Institute which helps co-ordinate and I thought it would be a very good idea if we had something similar here. So I wanted to try and see if I could set up something like that. I spent some time doing it, but ultimately it was a terribly difficult thing to do and it didn't get done. I also wanted to do more work abroad so I worked at the World Health Organisation in Eastern Europe, which I enjoyed very much.

Then you moved on to Consumers International

I became interested in consumerism as a kind of 'third way' in so far as the idea of state control of industry or commerce in order ensure fairness and equality was clearly not on the agenda; it wasn't going to happen. We were all in a free market now. I think we have to accept that. But the idea that the free market could be controlled and regulated to ensure as far as possible fairness, equity, and safety, that appealed to me. The idea that you have a strong consumer movement which is not part of private sector not part of the public sector, but an organisation where you campaign for safety standards and good access, I find that quite interesting.

This international federation, originally called the International Organisation of Consumer Unions and now called Consumers International, was set up to represent the consumer at the international level because more and more consumer issues are settled internationally rather than nationally. Its second job is to get consumer organisations started in the developing world. I found that attractive so I joined them and looked after the countries in the OECD. [Organisation for Economic Co-operation and Development]

That was fascinating because I got to travel a lot and also as I represented the OECD countries we had offices in Zimbabwe for Africa, Chile for Latin America and Malaysia for Asia. We had our Directors' meeting twice a year, always in one of those countries, so I got to see them and meet their people, which was a privilege. But working in the OECD countries where the main consumer issues are, for example, what's the best TV to buy, what's the best car, is a long way from the fundamental consumer issues which you get in the developing world. And after a while, I was a bit tired of travelling. I was out of the country one day in three. So I decided it was time to move on. But it had been great and I had made lots of friends in that movement all over the world.

How did you get your first job at the Millennium Commission?

I saw the advert for Director of Policy and Corporate Affairs. It suited me because I know how policy develops, I know how government works, I've been 'out there', I'm fairly streetwise and I'd had experience of the media. It fitted in.

And no regrets?

No. It's been a rollercoaster ride! We're an organisation with a limited life and we go through all the classic periods of organisational change but in five or ten years without middle age. So it's a dynamic organisation very rapidly changing. When I first joined I was working for the Director at the time, Jennie Page, a very able women, but she left after six months to go and build the Dome. So I took over from her. I had to learn a lot.

I'm managing an income of a million pounds a day, and 96 staff. Also my board is the only quango I know of with government ministers on the Board and more than that, with opposition politicians too. I've got Chris Smith, Mo Mowlam and Michael Heseltine and 6 independents. Politically, it's a unique situation. Keeping everybody together is a skill.

And also we're here to support Millennial projects, but there is no definition of what is Millennial. The other lottery quangos – arts, sports, heritage – have a common interest, but here we have everything from the New Millennium stadium in Cardiff to village halls to bridges to grants to individuals and the Dome. The diversity is huge.

Ideally, what would you like to do next?

I'm not sure. I've never had a long-term plan. At each stage in my career there comes a time when I feel the desire to move and do something else. Partly reflecting my consumer background, the idea of regulation interests me. Perhaps financial services where I think the industry could perform better. But I don't really know. My family background never encouraged me to be explicitly ambitious, I never thought I would get a degree or anything like that, so I don't have a huge amount of direction, yet clearly something internal drives me on. I suppose there are good and bad points about that.

Good and bad about not having 'a hugh amount of direction'? Such as?

The bad points are that you may not achieve as much as you could have done. You don't push yourself in a certain direction and go out and grab opportunities; you don't prepare yourself for things. It's more of a drunken walk, you do this, that, this way, that way. It's not a straight road you're on. On the good side, however, the lack of tramlines makes you very flexible and able to react and respond and have an open mind. And the meandering part of your career may enable you to pick up lots of experiences which may make you particularly well qualified for jobs.

If my career has been somewhat meandering I am able to draw on experiences from such a wide variety of backgrounds and fields that I think I'm a good generalist. The older I get the more important experience and judgement becomes; judgement of people and situations. I know as you get older you can't compete with a 20-year-old in terms of sheer intellectual power or enthusiasm, the only thing you can bring is your experience and I have gained a very wide range.

If you were now talking to 21 year olds what would you say?

Would I say do as I do? I don't know. Job environments do change, technology changes, the need for re-skilling. Whether I could seriously say to people be like me and do this, do that, take your chances; I'm worried that might be a little bit irresponsible. I have achieved quite a lot but there has been luck along the way; you might not have that luck. I've also not had any responsibilities, I haven't had a family and I think I couldn't have taken some of the risks I did take if I had. So I think I'd have to be quite cautious in my advice. But I would urge people to aim high and not to take no for an answer. Try and balance the need for security and income with the importance of fulfilment in your job

6   Academia

There are some jobs that everyone thinks they know about, and university lecturer is one of them. The hostile stereotype usually goes along the lines of, 'well they do a bit of teaching – when they're not on vacation that is – but most of the time they're doing esoteric research which is all well and good for them, but precious little use in the outside world'. Even the positive stereotype usually emphasises the research side and the lack of time and organisational constraints. Undoubtedly, academics do have more freedom to organise their time around their timetabled commitments than many other professionals, a fact which is often cited by lecturers as one of the most appreciated aspects of the job, but whether academia could ever have been justly and universally described in 'ivory towers' terms is debatable. Certainly in recent years the 'real world' of funding constraints, productivity increases, evaluation and accountability has intruded forcefully into university life.

In the last 10 years funding per student has fallen by over a third, student numbers have doubled and governments have required more and more rigorous assessments of quality – both of teaching and research – and all this without a proportionate rise in staffing levels or, many would argue, a commensurate increase in salaries. The 1999 Independent Review of Higher Education Pay and Conditions (known as the Bett Report) acknowledged the situation.

Much of the substantial growth of the HE sector over the last decade has been
achieved through increased productivity…These changes have clearly put
greatly increased pressures on higher education staff…Certainly, evidence to this
Review indicated that both staff and institutions/ management believe that
jobs in higher education are now significantly more onerous…Academic staff
are typically teaching more students, a greater proportion of whom require extra
support; the quality assurance arrangements put them under greater pressure to
sustain and improve course standards (and to demonstrate that they are doing

so through what many see as burdensome bureaucracy) . . . The general percep-
tion among both academic and non-academic staff is that the manifest increase
in their productivity over the last decade has gone wholly unrewarded.

But despite all this, and however much they may complain about the
interference of politicians, civil servants and, even more, the Quality
Assurance Agency, most academics would probably still admit that, on
balance, it remains a rewarding career. In order to counteract the
sometimes rose tinted view of budding academics, what follows may
appear to emphasise the more problematic or negative aspects of the job,
but I would want to stress that though the burdens may have grown,
there is still much satisfaction to be gained from teaching and research,
even if the third core role of administration is less appealing to many.

Teaching

How much teaching an academic does depends not only on their
seniority and role in a department, e.g. a head of department would
probably have a lighter teaching load to compensate for time spent on
management tasks, but also on the type of institution in which they
work. Informal conversations with staff in various Government and
Politics & International Relations departments revealed quite substantial variations between old and new universities. (In 1992 the
distinction between polytechnics and universities officially ceased but
as differences still remain it is useful to distinguish between them. Thus
ex-polytechnics are called 'new' universities or post-1992 institutions
and the 'old' universities are pre-1992 institutions.) The average weekly
timetabled commitment of lectures and seminars/tutorials in new
universities was around 12–14 hours, whereas in the pre-1992 institutions it was lower at between 5 and 10 with an average around 8 hours.
However, you must remember that these figures refer only to the
actual time spent with students in the classroom. The research and
preparation of material beforehand can involve many hours of work,
particularly for novice lecturers or those teaching new courses.

A lecture or seminar that goes well is a thing of joy; one that goes
badly is undoubtedly a very depressing experience. Of course, it may
be the lecturer's own fault if a session falls flat, but maybe not. If you

are a student or recent graduate, think back over seminars where no-one had prepared, no-one spoke and just stared at their feet. Pity the poor lecturer who fought valiantly but in vain to get any sort of response; their job satisfaction at that point would have been nil.

Group dynamics – why some groups work and other don't – have always been a difficult thing to pin down. Some seminar groups just seem to gel; the students' personalities complementing each other and everyone is interested in the subject. Others just don't come together at all, characters jar and interest may be minimal. Such differences have ever been thus, but, off the record, some experienced academics will say that as the numbers of undergraduates have increased, the motivation and ability of students has declined resulting in less informed participation and so less reward for staff. This may or may not be the case, but it is certainly true that students now come from a wider range of educational and social backgrounds and often bring differing expectations of higher education – what they want to get out of it and what they believe they need to do to succeed in it. All of this poses new challenges for staff in terms of course content and delivery and more emphasis is now placed on the training of new lecturers in teaching methods and curriculum development.

Teaching at postgraduate level mainly takes places in the old universities (though the new ones are catching up) and many staff find this the most satisfying. Seminars on masters programmes are included in the timetabled hours mentioned above, but the supervision of doctoral students (PhDs) is in addition to this. How many PhD students a lecturer takes on is largely at their discretion based on the areas of expertise in demand and how much time they want to devote to the work. PhD students are obviously highly motivated and they are also working at a level and on a subject area akin to that of the lecturer. This comparative equality can make for stimulating debate. However, because it is a one-to-one relationship sustained over a number of years and because doctoral students work very much on their own, they can come to depend heavily, sometimes too heavily, on their supervisor for feedback and guidance and the relationship may not always run smoothly.

Apart from formal teaching and supervising, most lecturers will have an 'office hour' or maybe two, when students can just turn up and discuss any issues of concern which can sometimes be of a personal rather than just a work nature. In some universities the formal personal tutoring or pastoral system still survives, i.e. each student is allocated a specific personal tutor to go to if they have any personal problems. But whether it is through the personal tutoring system or just via the office hours, dealing with issues that will affect a student's work but are not directly about teaching or learning can be time-consuming and sometimes difficult for academic staff. Of course, they can call on other professionals in the university, counsellors for example, but it can still be hard for some staff to deal with.

With teaching goes marking. Frequently mentioned as one of the least enjoyable aspects of the job, 'tedious' is the word most used to describe it. If you are a current student who has recently poured your heart and soul into an assignment or exam, then this may not be what you want to hear. But reading a single essay or exam script is one thing, reading 100 is quite another.

The actual number of pieces of work marked by any one individual will vary across courses and semesters and will also be affected by the teaching arrangements. For example, in some departments graduate students (usually doing PhDs) are employed to take undergraduate seminars and also do the marking for their groups. However, even here, lecturers will mark the exam scripts as well as the postgraduate assignments. Where graduates are employed, staff may get away with as few as 20 postgraduate essays per semester and up to 100–120 undergraduate exam scripts. Otherwise lecturers are required to mark anything from 20–100 undergraduate essays and a similar number of exam scripts per semester – and all within the space of a few weeks. Reading the same (or similar) thing over and over again is not the most stimulating of exercises, but staff have to remain focussed and unbiased in order to mark fairly.

Whatever the trials and tribulations, all the lecturers I spoke to said that they enjoyed the teaching role. Some preferred seminar or tutorial work to lectures and others vice versa, but all felt that the exchange of ideas, the need to re-think and update their own knowledge and the satisfaction of seeing students develop and succeed remains a challenging and fulfilling part of the work.

Research

Important though teaching is to academics, the opportunity to continue to explore their subject and contribute to the debates in their discipline is every bit as attractive, if not more so. In term-time, most departments (whether Government, Politics and IR or any other discipline) try to allow each member of staff one day a week free of teaching and other commitments to do their own research, though of course, 'events' can intervene. At Oxford, for example, where the terms are only 8 weeks long (compared to 11–13 at other institutions) finding research time outside of vacations can be difficult. The administrative tasks associated with academic life (more of which below) can also eat into the supposedly free day at any type of institution and as one lecturer at a new university pointed out, Sunday often ends up as the research day.

But, find time for research and the subsequent writing they must. Not only will their own success in terms of promotion and wider professional recognition often depend on their publication record, but so could the fortunes of their department. Every 4 years there is a Research Assessment Exercise (RAE) which is an external evaluation of the amount and quality of research in each department in every university. The result of this exercise affects the amount of money coming into the department/institution. A good rating – the maximum score is 5 – will not only bring the greatest reward in terms of government funding it will also preserve or enhance the department's reputation and may improve or maintain its position in the various published university league tables. This in turn will also help to generate income by keeping up student recruitment both domestic and international. The latter is particularly sought after, not least because of the higher fees paid by international students, and understandably, they will be more attracted to higher ranking universities.

All academics are therefore under immense pressure to publish and for those just beginning their careers who also have to prepare lectures and other teaching materials for the first time, it can be very stressful. Bob Borthwick, a Senior Lecturer in Politics at the University of Leicester with 38 years experience in the profession, is all too aware of this. 'We're very conscious that the younger people in the Department have to make their mark and get publishing. Initially we try not to burden them with too much administration and aim to give them a lighter teaching load. There's an awful lot of pressure on them to make sure they've got the appropriate number of boxes they can fill in when it comes to the RAE.' Feeling the pressure first hand is Cécile Fabre. Following a first degree in France, a masters in Political Theory from York, a PhD from Oxford and three years postdoctoral research, she is now less than a year into her first lecturing post in the Department of Government at the London School of Economics (LSE). 'I think that the emphasis on publishing is one of the defining shifts in the profession in the last ten years. You have to have 4 pieces every 4 years for the RAE.' There is no hard and fast definition of what constitutes a 'piece' of work, but there is a definite hierarchy of quality as Cécile explains. 'Guidelines vary from one assessment to the next, but basically a book with a very good publisher like the Oxford University Press or the Cambridge University Press would be top. Next to that would be articles in refereed journals [i.e. journals which require the draft article to be submitted to two experts for comment before publication]. An article in a very good refereed journal would probably count for as much as, say, a monograph with a less prestigious academic publisher.'

Depending on the subject specialism your research may or may not require extensive and expensive trips to libraries and archives, governmental or non-governmental organisations at home or abroad etc. Not only will this eat into time allocated for the other aspects of the job, but it will also require funding. Some universities/departments are more generous with research money than others, but often you will need to apply for funds to external research councils and other bodies. Such applications are often lengthy and time-consuming, though obviously worth the effort if you are successful.

Quality of work has always been important in academia, but now there is the added burden of quantity, so while research still remains one of the most attractive aspects of the job, it also brings some of the greatest pressures.

Administration

This is the bane of most lecturers' lives. If you really want to spoil their day just ask them about it! Of course, there have always been tasks unrelated to teaching or research and meetings to decide on exam questions, agree final marks, discuss future teaching programmes, organise internal, practical matters etc., not to mention paperwork, but again in the last ten years or so the volume has grown considerably. One of the major sources of both meetings and form-filling is the periodic teaching quality assessment by the Quality Assurance Agency. It just so happens that this academic year (2000/2001) it is the turn of Politics and International Relations departments to be QAA'd, as they say. At Staffordshire University the visit will take place in November 2001 but weekly meetings of all staff have already been going on for almost a year and as Lecturer Mike Brereton explains 'You're generating audit trails that go back two years and there are very significant documents to be written. We're burning rainforests on a gigantic scale.' The University of Leicester has already been through their QAA visit and whilst they did well, it was, as Senior Lecturer Bob Borthwick points out, 'an enormous amount of effort and vast amounts of paper were involved to make sure we jumped through the appropriate hoops. A certain percentage of the things that we did will, I think, have permanent benefits, but an awful lot was a distraction diverting people's time from other useful things.' In response to universal complaints, it is planned to slim down future QAA requirements, but evaluation is an integral part of working life everywhere these days, so it will not go away. And, it does have important ramifications. As with the RAE, there is a grading system (maximum score 24) with the results being made public and affecting performance rankings, student recruitment etc.

The amount of time taken up by work other than teaching or research often comes as a shock to new entrants to the profession, including Cécile Fabre at LSE. 'It was one thing which I was very unprepared for and I think it is something which has to be stressed. As it happens, I'm the careers liaison officer in the department and I had to organise a careers day for all our students [another piece of admin.]. There was a session on academia and I pointed out to them that when they think of a lecturing job they think of teaching and research, but what they must realise is that about a third of the time is taken up with admin. It may sound like a joke but once a month we have to fill out a form saying how much of our time is spent on research, how much on admin. blah, blah, blah — and that takes another half an hour!'

Having said all that, some academic staff, particularly in the new universities, enjoy and use the administrative role as a route to promotion. Indeed, in all types of institutions, many of the most senior positions in the university, including Vice Chancellor, are normally held by academics who have usually worked their way through the hierarchy (Head of Department, Dean of School etc.). But there are also many in the academic community who would probably agree with Cécile when she says, 'Academia in this country has become more and more professionalised in a sort of quasi-managerial way and that doesn't fit in very well with the kind of people who go into it. They are often very independent and individualistic. It is sometimes very frustrating to have to comply with various governmental recommendations couched in management-speak.'

Outside activities

It is important to make and keep contacts with academics in other universities. Not only can the interchange of ideas stimulate new thinking, but also, on a more practical level, it can lead to learning about job, research or publishing opportunities. Most disciplines have their own organisations which can act as a focus for networking. In Politics it is the Political Studies Association which publishes journals and organises conferences amongst other things. Conferences provide a forum for meeting up with like minds and giving papers at them is a useful addition to a CV.

Depending on your area of expertise there are other opportunities outside academia which whilst they may not add greatly to your income, will almost certainly add interest. Think tanks and the media (broadcast and press) often welcome contributions from academics and there are more specialist niches, for example Special Adviser to a House of Commons Select Committee or government backed research. Experts on international subjects could also be called in as consultants to overseas governments or non-governmental organisations.

But before you can start trading in on your position, you have to get into the profession.

Getting in

To become a university lecturer on a permanent contract you will need a good BA/BSc (a first or upper second), a doctorate, possibly a period on a fixed-term research contract and/or possibly a temporary lectureship but definitely some publications.

Akin to many other professions, fixed-term contracts comprise a larger slice of employment than 15 or 20 years ago. It is something that concerns staff and their unions, not just because of the insecurity for those lecturers concerned, but also because it can lead to added work for permanent staff as their temporary colleagues may not be able, or indeed want, to get fully involved in longer term planning and anyway some of their time will have to be spent looking for their next job. Having said that fixed-term contracts still comprise only a minority of all contracts, but it is worth bearing in mind that you can't take an immediate permanent contract for granted when you're doing your career planning.

Getting a good degree is obviously the aim of all higher education students, but it is an absolute necessity if you want to go on to become an academic, not least because it will influence your chance of getting funding for your higher degree(s) – more of which below. Though it may be possible to go straight from a BA or BSc onto a doctorate (PhD), the majority of students these days will first do a masters (either an MA or an MSc) usually on a full-time basis which takes one year, or sometimes part-time over two years. The masters involves taught courses, essays and a dissertation of anything from ten to twenty thousand words. Ideally it should also cover training in research methods. Courses are listed in various directories which you will find in your university Careers Services as well as on the internet. A couple of references are in the Further Information section at the end of this chapter. Application is direct to each course (there is no clearing house like UCAS for undergraduate courses) and while there is often no specific closing date, it is best to get your applications in around January/February in the final year of your degree or even earlier for the top ranking universities.

Though PhDs will also involve some training in research methods, they are basically pure research on a subject of your choosing culminating in a book-length thesis which should be an 'original contribution' to the scholarship of the area. Normally, doctorates take 3 to 4 years on a full-time basis and 5-7 years part-time. Application is direct to the institution and in deciding where to take your PhD you need to bear in mind the calibre and nature of the research interests of the staff in the department. As you will have seen in the above discussion of teaching, the role of the supervisor is crucial, so it is important that you respect their work. If you are in any doubt about the best place to study, discuss it with your current lecturers who will know, or be able to find out, about suitable departments for your area of interest.

Theoretically you could go straight into a permanent lectureship at the end of your PhD, and some people do. But others, either through choice or necessity, will take up a fixed-term research post first. Whether voluntary or forced, this experience will enhance their CV and allow them time to produce work for publication including, perhaps, their PhD thesis. It is so important to get into print and an early start is essential to impress future employers. Finally, temporary lectureships provide more experience of all aspects of academic life and can be the stepping stone to the Holy Grail of a permanent lectureship.

Funding

So, where does the money come from to take you through this long apprenticeship? Obviously as a temporary lecturer or a fixed-term contract researcher you will be paid a salary, but funding for masters and PhD can be more problematic.

What public funding there is for postgraduate study comes from the government via various research councils. The Economic and Social Research Council (ESRC) is responsible for Politics and International Relations, Economics, Sociology, Economic and Social History, Sociology, Social Policy, which are the areas most likely to be studied by people interested in politics in its broadest sense. Philosophy and aspects of history other than social and economic, are covered by the Arts and Humanities Research Board (AHRB) as well as all the other arts and humanities subject areas. Full details of their schemes, criteria, application procedures etc. can be found on their websites (addresses in the Further Information section) but briefly: – they both offer a limited number of studentships (i.e. grants, also called awards) for masters and doctoral study; they both assess applications on the basis of previous academic performance and referees' reports, and for research applications on the description of the project; they have closing dates in May and June; and competition is fierce. This academic year the AHRB had 1670 awards across all its subjects and at both masters and doctoral level. It received around 5,000 applications. So, only about a third of applicants were successful. The ESRC offered just 62 studentships for masters in Politics and International Relations although there are hundreds of students on such courses in the country. Of course, some universities will have their own scholarships and there are various trusts and charities you can apply to, but even so the vast majority of masters students are funding themselves which means paying for fees (minimum around £2,500) as well as living expenses. The ratio of success for PhDs, however, is much better. Again, in Politics and International Relations, 157 applications were received by the ESRC and 66 offers were made, i.e. a success rate of 42 per cent. Women comprised 36 per cent of applicants and managed to get 46 per cent of the offers and 2 of the 5 applicants over the age of 40 were successful. However, of the 73 applicants between the ages of 26 and 39, only 24 were successful compared to a ratio of 79:40 for the under 25s. How this distribution might change in the future, though, is unknown. From 2002, the ESRC will be moving to what they call the 1+3 system. It will still be possible to apply just for funding for PhDs, but otherwise candidates must apply for grants for the 4 years of a masters and PhD combined – there will be no money available just for masters courses.

Should you be lucky enough to get a grant, however, you will have your fees paid and a maintenance allowance (sometimes called a stipend) of between £7,500–£9,250 depending on whether you are studying in London or elsewhere and which Board/Council is paying.

If you are considering studying abroad, either at masters and/or PhD level, do take advice from experts in the field about which are the centres of excellence in a particular country. But as a starting point for information on courses and funding (which is different from above) look at www.prospects.csu.ac.uk which has information country by country.

When you are studying for your PhD, whether it be here or abroad, you might well have the opportunity to do some undergraduate teaching. This will not only augment your income but also your experience as Karen Small, a PhD student at Staffordshire University has found.

Karen Small – how to be a PhD student

After a false start on one degree, Karen worked in accountancy for a couple of years before returning to Essex University to take a degree in European Studies. Her A levels were in Maths, Further Maths, Physics and French.

I knew I wanted to do something involving languages, but not a straight language degree. I started learning Russian in my second year and because I would be spending my third year in Russia and wanted to know something more about the country, I took some modules in Russian Politics and thoroughly enjoyed them. I continued Russian Politics in the final year and did my dissertation on Russia and Nato relations [for which Karen got a distinction and won the departmental prize]. *I stayed on to do a Masters in Russian Politics and though it was good in many ways, it did involve more abstract political theory which I didn't particularly enjoy. After discussions with my tutor, I decided to research the 'Influence of the Russian Army on Foreign and Security Policy Making from 1991 to 1997' for my PhD.*

I applied to universities which were offering scholarships. My Mum – bless her! – had helped me through my masters and as long as I stayed in higher education I knew I would get support via a trust from my late father's employer, though it wouldn't be enough to support myself. But I took the place at Staffordshire not only because they were giving money for two years, but also because of the supervisor. He was a youngish member of staff who had only recently finished his own PhD but was very active in various research projects and good at attracting external funding. I figured that if I stuck with him it would be an opportunity for making contacts and getting involved in some of the projects – doing unpaid admin. stuff and getting to go to conferences. But then he left to go to another university. I was absolutely gutted.

It took me a while to settle down with a new supervisor and I was having some personal problems as well, but I was really helped by a member of staff at Keele University [not far from Staffordshire University] *who gave me support as well as some part-time work. I've been doing some undergraduate teaching at Staffordshire too which pays £25 an hour, which I really enjoy. It's fascinating finding out what the students do and don't know. You can see where people stand politically and it makes a change from just sitting in a room on your own all the time. I'm sure it's keeping me young too.* [Karen is 30]

What would I say to people thinking of doing a PhD? Well, it's completely different from anything you've done before. There's no structure to it. When you're doing a masters you've got lectures and seminars, but with a PhD, all of a sudden it's off you go and we want 80,000 words in three years time. Succeeding has less to do with how intelligent you are and more to do with the kind of personality you are -whether you've got the determination and self-discipline.

Network, make contacts. Everyone I know has had difficulties of one kind or another with their supervisors – personality clashes or just people leaving – so plug into networks as soon as possible to give you support. A lot of younger lecturers are very approachable and they'll take the time to help you if they can. Don't be afraid to ask for help. I made a lot of contacts via the Political Studies Association Graduate Network.

I really struggled initially trying to put anything down on paper. I knew what I wrote wasn't likely to end up in that form, but somehow the act of starting to write was just so daunting. But though the thesis is the biggest thing you will ever have written, you're going to write far more throughout your academic life – and hopefully a whole lot better. The PhD is more like an initiation rite. It's a means to an end, not an end in itself.

It hasn't always been easy, but I don't regret taking on the PhD, it's very satisfying – I just wish there were a few more jobs around!

The job market

Karen alludes to the fact that there is not an enormous number of jobs. Obviously there are only a finite number of universities in the country and movement of staff between them can be quite limited. Plus, of course, given the number of specialisms in each discipline, not every job advertised will be appropriate. A good source of vacancy information on the internet is http://jobs.ac.uk and picking a week at random (March 2001) and searching on Politics, 15 jobs came up. Two were for research assistants, two for temporary lectureships, and two for senior posts. Of the permanent lectureships the subjects being sought included International Relations with special reference to conflict analysis; Institutions and Development with special reference to institutions, policies and politics of environmental sustainability; Public Policy and Administration; Political Theory; Political and Cultural Geography of the Former Soviet Union; and European Politics. So, as well as being able to teach on more general courses, lecturers are chosen by their specialism which will inevitably limit the field of applicants. Whilst this restricts the number of jobs you could apply for as a new lecturer, on the positive side it means that the number of your competitors will be similarly limited.

The main reason for choosing a particular specialism and PhD topic will, of course, be your interest in the subject. But, on a practical level, it will help if your interest can coincide with an area which is popular with undergraduates and has the potential to attract research funding. That way you will be doubly saleable in the jobs market. By the time you start thinking about your masters subject you will probably have a sense of the growth areas in your discipline which may inform your choice.

Terms and conditions

How much you earn as a lecturer will depend on which type of institution you work in as pre- and post-1992 institutions have slightly different pay scales. A new pay deal has just been negotiated by the unions – primarily The Association of University Teachers (AUT) for old universities and the National Association of Teachers in Further and Higher Education (NATFHE) for the new ones – and from February/March 2002 the nationally agreed scales will be as follows. In new universities the Lecturer scale is £19,575–£26,686 and Senior Lecturer £24,906 to £32,910. The old university equivalents are Lecturer A and Lecturer B which are £20,470–£24,435 and £24,455–£32, 537 (plus discretionary points up to £36,355). The highest nationally agreed scales are Principal Lecturer in the new universities and Senior Lecturer in the old and go up to a maximum of £39,141 and £41,732 respectively. Professors and other senior posts are negotiated individually by each institution. If you're aiming for the top, Vice Chancellors currently earn between £80,000 and £150,000 depending on the size of the institution.

The fabled holidays are not quite as people think. In new universities there is a contractual standard of 35 days plus Bank Holidays but the old universities each have their own rates. However, as you might realise by now, vacations are a prime source of research and writing time and not to be frittered away.

In conclusion

Academic life is a mixture of opposites – highly individual and reflective work interspersed with periods of public exposure. Though there is sometimes collaboration with colleagues, for most academics research and writing are essentially solitary activities whereas publishing lays bare your work to a critical readership and teaching and giving papers at conferences require a public performance. Obviously not every lecturer will be equally good at all aspects of the job, or indeed enjoy all equally, but they must at least perform adequately in each area.

All the lecturers I spoke to felt they had made the right choice, even those who have been in the profession for many years and seen changes of which they don't wholly approve. But, if you are considering academia as a career, remember it will take time, money, self-belief and determination. It is a worthwhile, but by no means easy option.

Summary   **Academia**

Role	• Teaching and tutorial guidance, research and other forms of scholarly activity, examining, curriculum development, administration
Requirements	*Education*: First degree, higher degree (usually a doctorate)
	Nationality: Any
	Age Limit: None
Equal opportunities	• Applications welcome from all

Relevant work experience: Teaching experience an advantage

- Publications preferred

Selection Procedure

- Posts advertised (as and when vacancies) in *The Times Higher Education Supplement*, quality newspapers, relevant specialist journals and at http://jobs.ac.uk

- Selection via application form and interview, plus any of: lecture, presentation, written submission of work

Key Skills and Qualities

- Ability to put across complex information and concepts both in writing and orally. Research skills. Self-motivation and discipline. Organisational ability.

Pay and Conditions

- Scales from Spring 2002:

Old universities:
Lecturer A: £20,470–£24,435
Lecturer B: £25,455–£36,355
Senior Lecturer: £34,158–£41,732
Researcher 1B: £17,726–£19,681
Researcher 1A: £17,626–£26,491
Researcher II: £24,435 – £36,355
Researcher III: £30,819 – £41,732

New universities:
Lecturer: £19,575–£26,686
Senior Lecturer:. £24,906–£32,910,
Principal Lecturer:. £31,129–£39,141
Researcher A: £11,562–£16,008
Researcher: £16,905–£25,793

Hours: In new universities contractual maximum of 18 hours a week. Individually negotiated in old universities.

Holidays: In new universities standard of 35 plus statutory holidays. Individually negotiated in old universities.

Promotion: By individual submission and dependent on policy and financial situation of the individual institution.

Job security: Good for those on permanent contracts

Political activities: No restrictions on external political involvement

Further Information

- For lists of masters and some PhD opportunities see *Directory of Graduate Studies* or any of a number of similar directories in your university careers service or search on www.prospects.csu.ac.uk
- Information on the main public funding bodies is at www.esrc.ac.uk (Economic and Social Research Council) and www.ahrb.ac.uk (Arts and Humanities Research Board)
- Two very useful books on academia as a career are: Blaxter, L., Hughes, C., Tight, M., *The Academic Career Handbook.* The Open University Press 1998 and Ali, L., Graham, B., *Moving On In Your Career.* RoutledgeFalmer 2000

7   Think tanks and pressure groups

Think tanks

What is a think tank? That's not an easy question to answer. The term is often used quite loosely to describe all sorts of groups looking into any social and/or political issues. It's probably impossible to come up with a watertight definition, but certainly the aim of all so-called think tanks is to publish high quality research and proposals that will inform and influence public policy debate. In that, they share some common ground with each and any of academics, pressure/interest groups, government policy units/task forces and, even, party political organisations. However, unlike academics the work is rarely, if ever, done for its own sake and think tanks place a strong emphasis on readability and the publicising of their findings. Unlike many pressure or interest groups, the areas of concern to think tanks are often wider than one particular issue. And, whilst government policy units and task forces are of a limited lifespan and tied directly to government, think tanks are permanent and independent organisations. Finally, though they usually have a specific political (with a small 'p') bias or may even be identified with specific parties, think tanks are not formally part of those organisations, though the Fabian Society is affiliated to the Labour Party. So, research, policy proposals, usually from a particular political perspective, accessibility and widespread dissemination of their reports and publications etc. typify the work and approaches of think tanks.

By far the majority of think tank publications are produced by academics, or other experts in particular fields, including politicians. Most work is commissioned and quite a lot is provided free by the authors. What this means, in terms of employment, is that most think tanks have very small permanent personnel and even fewer of these will be researching and writing. For example, the Centre for Policy

Studies has six full-time members of staff, Politeia four, The Centre for Reform just two and the John Stuart Mill Institute relies wholly on volunteers. The Policy Studies Institute (PSI), the Royal Institute of International Affairs (RIIA), Demos and the Institute for Public Policy Research (IPPR) are amongst the largest organisations, but even they only employ between 30 and 60 people, many of whom are involved primarily or wholly in administration of publications and organising conferences etc. At the PSI there are approximately 25 researchers at different levels of seniority and at the RIIA there are just 15 in-house researchers at any one time and those on one to two year fixed term contracts. In these organisations, researchers will normally need to have a previous track record of research and publication.

However, all is not lost for new graduates and those with masters degrees. There are some opportunities to work on research, at least as part of the job. At IPPR for example, Research Assistants will work on their own projects but also assist more senior researchers by doing their supporting administration. Will Paxton graduated from LSE with a degree in Social Policy in 2000 and is now working on two projects in the Social Policy team. 'I'm looking at pensions and long-term care. I do most of the administration on that and a fair amount of the research, though we do commission a lot. I'm also working on another project called Assets which is looking at trying to build up people's asset base rather than just concentrating on increasing income. You might have seen items in the press about the Baby Bond – giving children £1000 at birth – that's one of our ideas.'

At Demos – whose stated aim is 'to reinvigorate public policy and political thinking and to develop radical solutions to long-term problems' – is Rachel Jupp who also joined straight from her degree (Social and Political Sciences from Cambridge).

As a researcher I probably spend about 60 per cent of my time researching, 20 per cent admin. stuff – that's my own administration but also organising events and seminars – and the other 20 per cent doing project management. I do quite a lot of speeches for conferences, seminars and training events. Think tanks are definitely on the conference circuit and one of the areas I specialise in, education, is particularly in demand. Last week I did an event for Design Education Week which was promoting creativity in education. Also I did a training session for people interested in working in the media as well as a briefing for American journalists about British politics.

Because of the emphasis on dissemination of their work in order to influence policy decisions, think tanks will want to get involved in the areas mentioned by Rachel, plus they will often seek to promote their publications through all the mass media – press, radio and television. Staff must therefore be prepared to promote the work and the organisation as well as do the behind the scenes research and writing.

Skills and Qualities: As with all high-level research, think tank work requires well-honed analytical skill and the ability to marshal large amounts of complex information. In addition you need the writing and presentation skills to put the results across in an accessible way. Because a fair amount of the time is spent on arranging presentations, conferences and publications, organisational skills and the ability to work under pressure are also important. Intellectually, think tanks can be high-octane environments so you will need to have confidence in your own ability and ideas.

Ways in: Senior researchers will need to have higher degrees and/or a research and publication track record, but the best way in at graduate level is via voluntary work, known as internships. Most think tanks, however small, will have people coming in on a voluntary basis, certainly to do administrative work. However, in the larger ones, particularly if you can give a fair amount of time, you might well have the opportunity to get involved in research projects. Once you are known in the organisation, your chances of being offered a paid position when one arises are much greater. Both Rachel and Will had been interns with their respective think tanks before and during their degree studies. To apply just send in your CV. However, the bad news for everyone, particularly those who do not live or study within travelling distance of these exclusively London based organisations, is that internships are rarely, if ever, paid.

And thereafter: Contracts in think tanks are often short-term, but in any case many junior researchers will stay only a couple of years before choosing to move on to other things. And it is a good thing to have on your CV; think tankers have gone into many of the areas covered in this book. Plus, if the political flavour of your think tank is in tune with the government of the day, so much the better!

Summary **Researcher/Research Assistant**

Role	• To undertake research, disseminate findings and give administrative support to other projects and senior researchers
Requirements	*Education*: Good degree, usually in any discipline though certain subjects may be specified for particular posts
	Nationality: None specified
	Age limit: None specified, though most entrants are in their 20s
	Equal Opportunities: Open to all
	Relevant work exp. Voluntary work, i.e. internships, distinct advantage
	Postgrad. qual. Masters useful but not required (for Senior Researcher posts PhD usually required)
Selection Procedures	• Posts may be advertised in the *Guardian*, *New Statesman* or specialist journals
	• CV and interview(s)
Key Skills and Qualities	• Research, analytical, written and presentation skills
Pay and conditions	• Vary between employers. Average starting salary range is approximately £17,000–£20,000.
	• Hours, holidays etc. by negotiation
	Promotion: Possibly to senior researcher, but most people will move on after a year or 2.
Further Information	• See individual websites. There are links to many of them from the Politico's Resources page at www.politicos.co.uk

Pressure Groups

As with think tanks, there is no precise definition of the term 'pressure group', though in academic circles there has been some debate about it. As a hapless Careers Adviser, I use the term in rather cavalier fashion to mean organisations set up specifically, or mainly, to exert pressure on legislators (and possibly other groups with power) on specific issues – anything from animal protection, civil liberties, gay rights or environmental concerns to international human rights and domestic constitutional reform. Whilst pressure groups will differ in the areas of interest, organisational structure and size (most are very small), there are often similarities in terms of employment.

For a start, many people will choose to work for such organisations because they identify with the aims and want to be part of bringing about change. They certainly won't be doing it for the money. Most pressure groups have limited incomes, and staff salaries are usually low in comparison to jobs of comparable responsibility in the commercial sector. Starting salaries are anywhere between £12,000 and £17,000, and that's in London. Also, many employees will have started off as volunteers. A lot of pressure groups could not function without voluntary help, but the process is two-way. Volunteers gain valuable experience that they can then use to get a paid job within the organisation or move into employment elsewhere. The more time you can give as a volunteer, the more likely you are to be involved in the interesting and challenging work of the group.

Anna Stenning (degree in Philosophy from King's College London) finds her time in the London Press Office of Amnesty International UK (human rights) provides valuable experience. When she returned from a year out in Spain after her degree, she knew she wanted to work in the voluntary sector and went the rounds of various employment agencies who specialised in the area. They all told her how hard it was to get into that type of work without experience, so she decided to get it. 'I started doing three days a week and worked on press cuttings – surveying the press every day for human rights related stories and mentions of Amnesty International. Then I went on to do press logging of other coverage on our database, taking media calls and general enquiries about Amnesty's work and learning how to write press releases. Recently I've been involved in a project to put together a briefing on the situation in Macedonia. This was about a month's work and I researched all the relevant areas: the principal players, other NGOs and government involvement.' Anna is also now doing some paid work acting as administrative support and liaison point for Amnesty's local groups and activists in the UK.

Most of the research for Amnesty is provided by the International Secretariat which is just down the road from the UK division. The campaign advisers there specialise in particular geographical areas of the world and will have joined the organisation with specialist knowledge, perhaps from higher degrees, and with relevant experience. However, in many pressure groups the roles are not so specialised and will involve administration, general campaigning and/or media work.

Helena Moor is a Campaigns Co-ordination Assistant at the environmental group Friends of the Earth (FOE). She originally started with the organisation as a volunteer after her masters in Conservation (first degree in Biology). Half her job is as Personal Assistant to the Campaigns Director and the other 50 per cent as a Campaign Assistant. This involves co-ordinating all the groups participating in the current European GM (genetically modified food) campaign and being the central point of contact, as well as distributing campaign action packs. A lot of the work is administration but she also gets involved in compiling the campaign materials and writing briefings, mainly for MEPs, MPs, the public and local and regional FOE groups.

At Charter 88, which is concerned with political reform in the UK, Araba Webber (degree in Modern History and Politics from Sheffield) is the Local Groups' Officer and one of 12 staff. She originally joined the organisation as Receptionist and chose it rather than a job in the commercial sector because, as she puts it, 'I wanted to work in something that I cared about and thought was important.' She's been in her current post for 6 months. 'We have a network of local groups and activists around the country and my job involves helping them to campaign locally. For example during the general election, a lot of the local groups ran public meetings with all the parliamentary candidates and we've also run campaigns in the past around proportional representation for local government. I co-ordinate meetings, make sure they have all the material they need. I produced a campaign pack which included model letters to MPs to find out their views on electoral reform, model press releases, information on how to run a public meeting, information on the best way to get a response from your MP and so on. We also produce a local groups newsletter usually every 2 or

3 months, though it was more frequent in the run up to the election.'

The Confederation of British Industry (CBI) which describes itself as a lobbying organisation on behalf of business, is one of the larger groups having around 220 staff and is unusual in that it doesn't rely on volunteers and takes on new graduates directly into policy adviser roles. There are currently 15 new graduates, one of whom is Maniza Ntekim who is Policy Adviser in the Learning and Skills Group which covers education and training from primary school through higher education and into workforce development. She has a degree in Politics, Philosophy and Economics from Oxford and a masters in International Politics from the School of Oriental and African Studies in London. The selection process for the job involved looking at papers produced by the CBI and the TUC (Trade Union Congress) and having to argue from the former's point of view. In fact, she is now working on a joint CBI/TUC productivity initiative looking at ways of raising the skills level of the workforce as a way of improving productivity. 'Another large part of my brief is schools – standards, ways to improve education and business links etc. – as well as looking at skills shortages, where they occur and how they can be addressed. Writing briefing papers is a large part of the work and because we are coming up with policies on how to address problems, creativity is important. Although I'm part of a small team, I have to work on my own initiative and have confidence in my own ideas.'

Promotion at the CBI is to Senior Policy Adviser, in the other organisations it will depend on their structure and size. Whilst the promotion prospects may be limited and the money not terrific, for Araba there are definite advantages to working in a pressure group: 'Whatever role you do there's always other things you can be doing. There's a lot of scope for development and trying new things. It can be a good training ground if you want to move on to other things.'

Most groups now have websites on which they will advertise any job vacancies and they might also use the *Guardian* and other quality papers, particularly for jobs in research, media/communications and public affairs which will require relevant experience. However, as we've seen, volunteering is one of the best ways of getting in. As many of the HQs of pressure groups are in London and the South East it does put people outside that area at a bit of a disadvantage. But, as many organisations have local groups and activists, you can always get involved at this level.

The sector is so varied that a summary would need to be so general as to be of little use. The best way of finding out about the work and opportunities is get involved with groups aligned to your interests. Find out more about them by looking at their websites.

Interview **Iain Dale**

Iain Dale is the Managing Director of Politico's Bookstore and Publishing. He started out as a researcher for an MP and subsequently worked in parliamentary affairs, specialist journalism and lobbying. He is now a regular broadcaster on radio and TV.

CV

Education	BA (Hons) German, University of East Anglia
Career	1985–7: Personal Assistant and Campaign Manager for Patrick Thompson MP
	1987–9: Public Affairs Manager, British Ports Federation
	1990 Public Affairs Consultant
	1990 Insurance Reporter, Lloyds List
	1990–6: Deputy Managing Director, The Waterfront Partnership
	1996– Managing Director, Politico's Bookstore and Publishing

Did you come from a political background?

No, my parents were farmers. I think it was my grandmother that got me interested in politics. I can remember in the 1974 election when I was 11 walking into my parent's bedroom having written a few paragraphs on why you should or shouldn't vote for each party. My mother rolled over and told me to go back to bed! My parents were sort of conservative, wet conservative, though they voted Liberal in 74.

When I went to university I fully intended to be a German teacher or teach English abroad but my interest in politics grew. I started the

University's first Conservative Association and went out campaigning in the '83 election, and missed most of my lectures.

How did you get the job as MP's researcher?

I knew Patrick Thompson, the MP for Norwich North because I'd helped quite a lot in his election campaign. I knew he didn't have a researcher, just a part-time secretary so we arranged to meet one afternoon and talk it over. That was in the autumn of my final year. He suggested I spend a week with him in the Commons just before Christmas to see if I liked it and that went very well. I was one of the first in my year to get a job.

MPs didn't get very high allowances then so it was very badly paid. Moving to London and having to exist on about £6,000 a year was no joke. That's changed now, the allowances are higher though a lot of MPs still treat their staff as wage slaves.

Do you remember your first impressions?

For the first few weeks you're totally in awe of the place. I remember on my second day walking along the corridor and Jim Callaghan and President Ford were walking in the other direction. You think 'what am I doing here?' But after a few weeks it becomes like any other place to work, well almost. To this day, there is still a little bit of magic when you walk in the building. It was a great place to work in terms of atmosphere and terrible in terms of facilities. My office was in the basement of one of the buildings a couple of minutes walk away. I shared it with two other MPs' secretaries. We had no storage space and we had to buy our own computer.

And what did you actually do?

I spent a year working in the House of Commons and if I'm honest it was more as a secretary than a researcher. I didn't do any speechwriting. it was mainly constituency work. We would regularly get 100 letters a day and many of them meant you had to write two or three letters as a result; an acknowledgement to the constituent, one to the relevant local council or government department, and then back to the constituent once you'd got what they needed. Some constituency casework can go on for years. Sometimes Patrick would dictate a reply, but generally I would write it, and type it, and he would sign it, so I had a lot of autonomy.

One of the frustrations of the job was dealing with the letters, probably about half of them, that really should have been directed to the local councillor, social services or one of the other agencies. But you can't write back and say 'sorry, not me' because that would give a bad impression and it was a marginal seat. And then there were the absolute nutters! You'd get people saying that the government was trying to put radiation through their house and the rays were going to get them and that sort of thing. Or, would Mr Thompson please go round and fix their washing line.

After a year, when the election wasn't far away, it was decided I should actually base myself in the constituency. It was a very marginal seat and regarded as key, so I was partly paid by Conservative Central Office and my task was to work with the local party agent and get the campaign going. Though Patrick didn't have a high national profile, he was well known as a constituency MP and we highlighted this in our campaign. We targeted people with direct mail and introduced telephone canvassing which had never really been done before in British elections. A lot of the work was going to local Conservative meetings and giving the members pep talks and encouraging them to get involved. Schmoozing! Anyway, our campaign seemed to work and helped the majority up from 1,500 to 7,500.

How did you plan your next move?

My whole life was consumed by this election campaign; getting in the office at 8 in the morning and not leaving until 9 or 10, so I didn't have much time to think about the future. But I knew that after it there was little point in me staying on, if I did it would just be very repetitive. When the election was over I took a well-deserved holiday and went to America for a month. One day I bought a copy of The Times and saw the advert. for Public Affairs Manager for the British Ports Federation and the National Association of Port Employers and I sent them my CV.

I had two interviews and they went really well. Then they wanted *me to go to the Conservative Party Conference in Blackpool, I think to see what I was like on a social occasion. They had all their Board there meeting MPs and I had to go and circulate. Anyway, I got the job. It turned out I'd beaten about 140 people to get it.*

What was it like working for two organisations?

I had a dual role. The British Ports Federation was the trade body for the whole industry. I had to produce a quarterly bulletin on all the political aspects affecting the industry. We'd organise meetings all over the country with local politicians. It was standard political PR work.

At the National Association of Port Employers I was employed specifically to lobby the government to get rid of the 'dock labour scheme' which gave dockers jobs for life and enshrined all sorts of restrictive practices. So over the next two years I spent a lot of my time devising a campaign to get rid of it, and that's what happened. We were highly successful. In April 1989 the Government announced plans to do it. I then spent the next 3 months doing the media relations side of the major dock strike which followed.

In a sense it was the making of me; it made me grow up. I knew that anything I said could have huge consequences not just for our members but for the country and the economy. There was one stage, I remember, the Sunday Times woke me up and said something about would you think about bringing in foreign dockers to work in the ports. I just said something fairly innocuous 'well, I suppose it's something we might consider at some stage' and they had that as their page one lead for that day 'Port Employers to Fly in Finnish Dockers'. It's one of those occasions when your heart sinks. But it actually proved to be the best thing that could have happened because it scared the trade unions; they couldn't actually believe that people they'd seen as very weak employers would already have plans to do this sort of thing.

Obviously, it wasn't just me. We had a group of 7 people who met every two weeks to review where we'd got to in the campaign. Each of us had our role and my function was to get the politicians on side and deal with the media. The others were a freelance journalist, a human relations specialist, two port people, two others from the office and

Nicholas Finney the Managing Director. They were fairly sparky meetings, hawks and doves, and it was interesting to watch the interplay between the two groups and how conflicts would get resolved. I really was thrown in at the deep end; in work at 6am and leave at 10pm, you were just running off pure adrenaline. It was a fascinating time.

Then in a sense, because we'd been successful in getting rid of the dock labour scheme, I'd done myself out of a job. There was no pressure on me to leave but again, like with the MP, I knew it had reached a natural end.

Was lobbying the obvious progression?

Yes. I had no particular desire to go into it, but it seemed the natural thing to do. I'd just run a very successful campaign, so I knew I was a marketable commodity. I contacted a head hunter and a few other people that I knew and was offered jobs at three different companies. I took the one at Charles Barker, a fairly large PR firm with a lobbying division and started on the same salary I'd been on at the Ports Federation, £25,000.

I was given a couple of clients: a car company and a campaign called Daylight Extra which wanted to change the time of day to give an extra hour of light in the morning in the winter. That one was quite interesting, but all the car people wanted was to have their pictures taken with Cecil Parkinson, Transport Minister at the time, which I could do but gave me no job satisfaction at all. I got very frustrated in a very short time. I would be sitting at my desk at 3 in the afternoon with nothing to do and I hated it. It's not what I was used to at all. I talked it through with the Managing Director and she tried to get me involved in other bits of the company, but it wasn't going to work out.

How did you get to Lloyds List?

I was talking to a journalist I'd got to know in the dock strike. I'd thought of journalism before, so, given my background, he said why don't you write to the editor of Lloyds List, the daily shipping, insurance and financial paper. I was offered a two-week trial and then a full-time job. I really enjoyed it, the only downside was they wanted me to be their insurance correspondent, about which I knew nothing and cared less! Though in the end I finished up writing a lot of their diary column and any political stories that came up. Then after 4 months I was approached by Nicholas Finney, my old boss at the British Ports Federation. He wanted to start a lobbying company and would I go in with him. He didn't want me to put in any money, but he would give me some equity. So I was faced with a real dilemma. I loved what I was doing in terms of writing, but the lobbying company had the potential to make quite a lot of money. I wavered but then decided to go in with Nicholas and we started Waterfront.

Given your previous experience of lobbying, why did you want to go back to it?

Waterfront was meant to be very different from general consultancies; we would specialise in areas we both knew something about, i.e. transport. In general consultancies you're a jack of all trades and expected to advise people on areas you don't understand, you take 6 months before you really understand your client's business. We knew about transport.

My main reservation was that I didn't think I'd be any good at business. I had no experience and I didn't regard myself as particularly entrepreneurial. I had assumed that running a business was all about making a profit, whereas actually it's all about managing a cashflow. I knew I could run an office and that I was reasonably good with people, but I had this thing about being no good at getting new business. But I found I was a lot better at it than I thought I would be. We started a separate conference company which was entirely me, and just before I left we started a publishing company, again entirely me. I learnt about the commercial world and about my own strengths and weaknesses. Unfortunately, I also learnt that friendship and mutual trust can sometimes count for little in business. For personal reasons, my time with Waterfront did not end happily, but I've got no regrets.

And so to Politico's...

Like any business, it has its problems, but I love doing Politico's. This job gives me what I need. I love all the media stuff that I do, probably all to do with ego! It challenges me on the business side and it's all my hobby. There aren't many people who do their hobby as their job.

You've moved around in the political world, but do you think people coming in now need to be more focussed?

I always have a deep mistrust of anyone who says in 10 years time I want to do this or that. You can't plan things like that. I wanted to be an MP but I lost interest in that a long time ago. Things just happen. Sure you've got to know what kind of things you want to be in but you can't plan it in detail. Anyway, a lot of the time you're governed by your financial needs. I went from nearly £80,000 a year at Waterfront down to a third of that at Politico's. But I'm willing to do that because I see this is a long-term investment. You can do all the planning you like but you never know what's going to turn up.

What sort of person should never work in the area of politics?

It depends which part. I would say don't get involved in it if you aren't very clubbable because politics is about clubs, factions. Also if your feelings are easily injured because there will always be people against you as well as for you and it's easy to think everyone's against you. I suppose if you're an adviser, working behind the scenes, you could get away with being a loner, but generally the most successful people in all aspects of political life are those who are fairly extrovert, who can get on with people even if they don't particularly like them. It is a bit of a two-faced business.

8   Public affairs (lobbying)

At its most basic, 'lobbying' means trying to influence the actions or decisions of those in power. As such it has a very long history; in fact, as long as there have been individuals or groups of people with power to affect the lives of others. Kings and queens, barons and squires would all have been lobbied by those beneath them in the power hierarchy. The modern form of professional lobbying, however, is largely a child of the 1970s and '80s. As good a definition as any, is that from a Civil Service guide to *Contacts with Lobbyists* (1999) which says that professional lobbyists '. . . whether individuals, partnerships or companies − [are those] who earn their living by providing their clients with contacts, information and advice about how to persuade the Government and other public sector bodies to do or give them what they want.'

There are two types of lobbyist, consultant and in-house, though whether either would refer to themselves by the name of lobbyist is debatable. Consultants will take on a number of clients on a fee-paying basis and will variously call themselves and their consultancies, political, parliamentary, public affairs or government relations consultants. In-house practitioners do just that; they are employed by one organisation and work solely for them usually under the departmental titles of public, parliamentary or political affairs.

Whoever they work for, the role of lobbyists is to understand the workings of the political system and identify the right people and the right method to get the right result for those who pay them. The result sought may be an immediate answer to a sudden development, a medium-term solution to an ongoing issue or a long-term plan to raise the profile and influence of the organisation on future political decisions. The right people may be MPs, or politicians in other Parliaments and assemblies, civil servants, European Commission staff, regulatory bodies, quangos or local government departments.

The right method will usually be a combination of approaches possibly involving direct contact with decision-makers or opinion-formers, media involvement, staging of one-off events, campaigning for and participating in public inquiries etc. In short, successful lobbyists need to know who's who and what works. As Michael Burrell, Chair of the Association of Professional Political Consultants, wrote in *Dod's Parliamentary Companion* (2001), 'It is accumulated common sense, rather than rocket science, but because it is what consultants do every day of their working lives, the best of them become very skilled in the most effective routes to success, rather as effective lawyers know how best to make a case in court.'

In order to be able to do this effectively, lobbyists need information on all the decisions, developments, events and future plans that may affect their employers' interests. In an age of information overload, monitoring it effectively and on a daily basis, is crucial.

Political monitoring

With the amount of information pouring out of Parliament and Government as well as other bodies such as think tanks, quangos and so on, keeping tabs on it all can become a full-time job. In fact, there are companies that specialise in just this, and in-house public affairs departments will usually buy in the services of such firms rather than allocate their own staff time to it. Large political consultancies may have their own dedicated team of staff to monitor, and the smaller firms will either buy in the service on behalf of their clients or allocate staff to the task on a rota basis. One such company is Portcullis Research where Account Executive, Natalie de Lima, alternates daily with another colleague. 'Say we had a client with an interest in soft drinks, then we would go through everything with a fine tooth comb looking for literally anything that could be relevant – companies' names, brand names, related issues like dental hygiene, sugar, packaging, recycling, etc. Essentially we monitor the *Vote Bundle* which is available each morning from the Parliamentary Bookshop. The *Vote Bundle* includes the *House of Commons Order Paper* with future business and parliamentary questions; the Commons *Hansard* with the previous day's debates, oral answers and written asnwers, plus the Lords *Hansard* and *Lords Minutes of Proceedings*. Whereas the *Hansard*s tell us what happened, the Order papers tell us what is going to happen and this is crucial. It gives clients time to respond to threats and opportunities identified through the monitoring process. We also go through the *Weekly Information Bulletin* and the *Lords Weekly Agenda*. This keeps us busy enough, but in addition to the Parliamentary papers, we need to monitor press releases, Ministers speeches outside the Commons and other political developments. We do use, the services of a press agency, which has access to the daily lobby briefings, and notice of Ministerial statements, Reports expected and so on. Plus, we check several websites during the day including the Central Office of Information, individual Deparmental sites and other relevant organisations which may relate to a client's business like the Food Standards Agency of the National Institute for Clinical Excellenc. There is an enormous amount of information to be sifted. Clients want information fast and depending on how much detail they require, the information is relayed by phone, e-mail or fax on a daily basis. Meanwhile other colleagues tackle EU sources. You could spend a full day just monitoring!'

Political Consultancy

A number of the large Public Relations companies will have Public Affairs sections, but there are also dedicated political consultancies. Listings of those that specialise in political consultancy are in Hollis *UK Press and Public Relations Annual* and *Dod's Parliamentary Companion*. Here you will find up to 25 firms advertising their services as Government Relations experts. A few concentrate on certain sectors and/or industries, for example, local government, transport, food and drink etc., and some have offices in the other decision-making centres of Edinburgh, Cardiff, Brussels and occasionally other foreign locations. As well as monitoring, they will offer other services including research and strategic advice. The majority are quite small, though they range in size from just a handful of staff, literally five or six, to a maximum of around 40 and while the terminology may differ slightly from firm to firm, the job titles are usually Junior Account Executive, Account Executive, Senior Account Executive,

Account Manager/Director: Catherine Rose is a Senior Account Executive at GJW BSMG Worldwide. Following a degree in Government and Public Policy from Newcastle Polytechnic and a Postgraduate Diploma in Industrial Relations from Warwick University she spent six years working in education, local government and a quango, the Training and Enterprise Council, in Greater Manchester, Merseyside and then London. All these jobs involved bidding for external funding, including European Social Funding, and positioning the organisations within local networks and partnerships. GJW were acting for her last employer, which is how she first came across them. Because they knew her and knew that they could work with her, the firm initially offered her a temporary post to cover maternity leave and then a permanent job.

Though Catherine draws greatly on her previous experience, not all her clients are public sector,

They are also private sector organisations who need to understand the view of the public sector. The issues raised can be something very localised, like a local planning decision, all the way through to assessing the ramifications of decisions taken in more than one country. Most clients come to consultancies because they've got a particular problem or there's an issue that's going to have an economic impact on them or prevent them developing. They'll say we think we need this type of support and you have to sit down with them and work out exactly what is they do require. It's all about assessing what the short-term needs are and then seeing how you can position them for the long term.

According to Catherine most Account Executives will have around 5 or 6 clients at any one time and will lead on 3 or 4, i.e. they will have primary responsibility for the account but will work with colleagues. In consultancies which have both straight Pubic Relations as well as Public Affairs arms, staff from both sides will often need to collaborate to give the client the service they require. Drumming up business for the consultancy is largely done by the Directors who use their own networks, but other staff are encouraged to follow up any contacts with new organisations they come across. It is important for all staff to be aware of the need to draw in new business. Athough some clients will stay with a firm for a number of years, the contract is constantly renewable. In other cases the consultancy may be on a one-off project fee, possibly with a success fee on top of that, or even hourly rate so attracting new clients is always a priority.

Getting In

Where a firm has both Public Relations (PR) and Public Affairs (PA) sections, it is possible to move from one to the other, but the direct entry level posts into PA are either into political monitoring or as a Junior Account Executive. In the latter, you would have some client contact but would mainly be assisting Account Executives and more senior colleagues by providing background research, organisation of events, meetings, media liaison etc. This is the time when you would be learning the business, but for the right people promotion to Account Executive can be swift.

Catherine Rose had extensive experience prior to getting her job, but it's not a necessity, and would not obviously be expected for Junior Account Executive. What most consultancies will look for in their new graduate recruits is interest and ability. Any degree discipline is acceptable, but Politics, Government, History or other social sciences show that you really do have an interest in the subject. Many recruiters would probably say that a year's experience as an MPs researcher/assistant is the ideal background. You would know the system and have some contacts already. In fact, a number of consultancies will advertise vacancies in the *House Magazine* (the Parliamentary in-house journal) precisely for this reason. However, others are happy to take on, or may even prefer, new graduates straight from university, as long as they can make themselves stand out. A good CV should show some relevant work experience during vacations, possibly in the media and some of the other areas covered in this book, or maybe a stage at the European Commission on graduating, party involvement etc. Your application should also demonstrate the ability to communicate with the sort of confidence and clarity you will need when dealing with clients. Though some consultancies will advertise any vacancies in the *House Magazine*, by far the majority of entry level jobs go through personal contact and speculative applications. The three firms that I spoke to all said they keep CVs on file and will go back to them when they have a vacancy. Occasionally they will use specialist recruitment agencies, though this method is more often used for the senior posts. A good source of vacancy information for Account Executive and up is www.publicaffairsjobs.com.

Salaries vary from firm to firm but for Junior Account Executive it seems to be anywhere from £15,000 to £20,000. However, promotion, on merit, can be swift and Account Executives could earn up to £23,000, Senior Account Executives around £25,000 and Account Managers up to £30,000 or £35,000 plus.

In-house Public Affairs

Though some may like the variety of clients in a consultancy, others prefer to be part of a specific organisation; to get to know a particular sector in more depth and know that they agree with its aims. All sorts of organisations will have their own public affairs people, from charities, though local government, to industrial assocations.

Below are three job advertisements published in the *Guardian* in early 2000. They span three areas – the voluntary sector, an industry body and a professional trade union. So, who got these jobs? What were their backgrounds and what do they do?

The National Council for Voluntary Organisations (NCVO)

Parliamentary & Campaigns Officer £21,157–£22,277 (pro rata 28 hours p.w.)

This is a crucial role within the Campaigns team and carries key responsibility for the success of integrating our MP Secondment scheme into parliamentary and campaigns work. You will also work closely with two other key Working Groups and will develop close, persuasive relationships with Civil servants, MPs, MEPs and Peers. Attendance at Party Political conferences will be an essential part of the role.

Success in this important post will demand considerable experience of working at a senior level with Government as well as the ability to assimilate and communicate complex concerns simply and concisely to politicians, civil servants and key opinion formers. Your three years plus lobbying experience will have given you an in-depth knowledge of Parliament and the political system as well as experience of organising events at Westminster and Party Conferences. The ability to manage a number of projects with multiple priorities is essential

---

The successful candidate was Richard Hebditch who has a first degree in History from Leeds and a masters in East European Studies from the

School of Slavonic and East European Studies which is part of the University of London (1995).

I didn't have a clear aim when I took the masters. I was interested in East European history anyway and it seemed like an excellent way of extending university life for another year. I was considering a PhD after, but when I finished the MA course I just wanted to go into a real job. But I didn't have much of an idea what job I did want, so for about a year and a half I did a range – voluntary work in a museum and for the National Campaign for the Arts (a pressure group), a bit of office work and other odds and ends. Then when the 1997 election was coming up I went home to Taunton and worked for the Lib Dem candidate on a voluntary basis. When she won the seat she employed me as her researcher at Westminster. I did that till 1998.

That sort of fixed my career in some ways; the work I've done since followed on. In May 1998 I got the job of Parliamentary and Policy Officer for a childcare charity, Kids Clubs Network, and stayed for about two years. It was quite a small operation, just 50 staff across the country, so the work was very varied but the core work was parliamentary. It wasn't a campaigning organisation as such, the aim was to keep MPs aware of the needs of after school childcare, keep the profile high. It was mainly done by letter campaigns and as part of an annual awareness raising week we tried to get MPs to visit an after school club in their constituency and actually ran one in the House of Commons itself.

The job at NCVO appealed to me because not only does the organisation have a higher profile but it covers a wider range of issues. One of the core parts of the work is running the MP secondment scheme whereby MPs spend time with a voluntary organisation. About 34 MPs have gone through it and it's a very effective way of lobbying because they get to see first hand how voluntary organisations work and what their interests and concerns are. It's my responsibility to organise it and make sure it runs smoothly. There is also an all-party group of MPs on charities and the voluntary sector which has regular meetings every 2 or 3 months. I work on that with the Head of our Campaigns Team. NCVO is also very keen on spreading good practice and sharing information around the voluntary sector, so we have a parliamentary workers group of about 60 members. I'm in charge of that. Then there's lobbying on specific issues. For example, not so long ago the Criminal Records Bureau was going to introduce charges for criminal record checks for volunteers. We campaigned on that and the Government agreed to give volunteers free checks.

Frustrations? I can't think of any. It's rewarding trying to be the voice of the members you represent. There's a lot of variety in the job and even though campaigns are planned in advance, things change and you have to act more spontaneously.

Chemical Industries Association (CIA)

Political Officer, Central London, Salary £25,000

A vacancy has arisen in our Public Affairs Directorate, reporting to the Head of the Political Office, for a highly motivated, intelligent and articulate self-starter to assist in the support of the CIA's representations to govenment and democratic institutions (especially the EU) and to politicians at all levels.

Ideally, you will be an Honours graduate (politics/public affairs preferred); politically non-partisan, with a sound grasp of EU and UK politics and procedure. You will also have experience of one or more of the following: researcher to MEP/MP; 'commercial lobbyist'; think tank work; EU/UK civil service; work within a political party HQ; legal experience, political journalism; experience of manufacturing industry.

You will need to have excellent drafting, communication, interpersonal and advocacy skills, be a good teamplayer and pay attention to detail.

Following two interviews, Elanor Cann was appointed. Her first degree was from Leicester University where she majored in European Politics and Italian and her masters in European Political Culture and Integration Studies was from Bath. Following this she did a stage at the European Commission which allowed her to see it all from the inside and, as she says, the experience certainly helped her to get a job in monitoring in a consultancy: 'When I got back from Brussels I just went through Hollis [a PR directory] and wrote to every single political consultancy in London that had a European desk.' That experience in turn allowed her to get the job at the CIA, though here all the monitoring is done for her by an outside firm. Her own work she describes as follows.

Working in a trade association that has a European Federation, we obviously have an office in Brussels that's made up of all the chemical trade associations in the EU. They have their own secretariat so a lot of the Brussels lobbying is done by them. We tend to concentrate on lobbying UK MEPs and also devel-

oping links with other UK nationals based in Brussels, for example UK Rep which is the Brussels office of the UK civil service.

Much of my work is representational which just means trying to improve our reputation with the opinion-formers in Government. Its about introducing ourselves to the key players and saying this is us, this is what we do and the benefit we give to society, employment and the general economy so that our concerns will be taken into account. Representation is an ongoing thing, twelve months of the year. It can take years to build up a good public image, but you can lose it in a day. This side of the work involves organising briefings on what we do. We might hold receptions in the House of Commons, meetings with members of relevant Select Committees, Ministers or government officials plus briefings in the European Parliament. I have admin. support for this, but I'm responsible for the overall strategy and logistical planning. The other side of the work is lobbying on a specific issue or piece of legislation. As soon as you know there's a piece of legislation coming up that you'd like to influence you immediately start lobbying specifically on that. If the ongoing representational work has gone well, you should already have the ear of the people who matter.

Royal College of Nursing (RCN)

Parliamentary Officer, £24,297 – £29,499

We need a highly motivated team player with three to five years' experience of working as a lobbyist in-house or in a consultancy or in parliament. The abilities to write clearly, analyse political change and grasp issues quickly are all vital. Knowledge about health services would be an advantage.

The RCN is the world's largest professional union of nurses. Its busy public affairs team undertakes high profile lobbying, media and campaign work on issues ranging from nurses' pay to long term care.

A graduate of English and American Literature from Warwick University (1997), Alexa Knight had always been interested in politics and active in local party politics. On graduating she moved to London and did a brief stint in general office temping. One of her placements was at Profile, a PR and Public Affairs consultancy where she subsequently went to work on a permanent basis. After a couple of months at a junior, admin. level she was promoted to Account Executive and then on to Account Manager.

I started doing straight PR, but a lot of the clients used the consultancy for both PR and lobbying, so I automatically started taking on more of the political side. Then I made a conscious decision to move into PA, though right up until I left I was still doing bits of PR. My clients tended to be small charities and overseas governments. The work included monitoring as well as the other aspects of account work. By that I mean the strategic planning – looking at the long-term needs of the clients as well as dealing with current issues. It was a very steep learning curve. The good thing about working in a small consultancy is that you get to move up quickly. The downside is that you might not always get the training you would in a large organisation.

After a while I just wanted a change, a different environment. The advantage of consultancy work is having different clients so the work can be quite varied. The pace tends to be fast and it's very results driven because you need to meet the needs of your clients. On the other hand, in-house you get to plan more long-term because you only have to answer to yourselves. You can be more strategic, there are more training opportunities, and on the whole, people tend to stay longer in the job. I made a conscious decision that I wanted to work for a not-for-profit organisation, so the RCN fitted the bill.

A typical week? Well, our week really starts on Friday which is when we see the diary for the following week in Parliament. If there are debates coming up that we think are relevant to us we may brief a politican – this could be by a phone call, a meeting or a written briefing. Or, if there's an ongoing inquiry by a Select Commitee we may give written evidence and follow up with oral evidence. In that case we'd ask our members, who would be nurses specialising in the relevant field, to meet the MPs and give evidence. Usually at the same time we'll have a proactive campaign going on aside from what's happening in Parliament. For example, at the moment we've sent our election manifesto to each Parliamentary candidate saying what we want to see the next Government do for health. So, there are several levels of activity.

The broad strokes of RCN's policy on various issues are decided by our members at the RCN's annual Congress, and at our AGM. Our role as Parliamentary Officers [there are 2 of them] is two-fold because we're the interface between Parliament and the RCN and our members. We monitor what's going on at an immediate level but we're also horizon scanning for what might be happening in the future. We like to keep our membership and the staff of RCN aware of what's happening. It's a two-way information process.

Skills and Qualities

Both consultancy and in-house work require the same general skills and characteristics: good written and verbal communcation skills; the ability to assimilate large amounts of complex information; interpersonal skills in the sense of being able to relate to a wide variety of people in different professional and social settings – from a public inquiry to a cocktail party; the ability to work on your own initiative and under pressure and, finally, to be able to work as part of a team.

As in-house Public Affairs' departments rarely, if ever, take on people with less than a couple of years experience, they also require a thorough knowledge of political processes and procedures and experience of briefing politicians, the media etc. Working in the European arena it is also important to have a good grounding in how the institutions work and a foreign language, though not essential, can be very useful. As Elanor Cann (CIA) says, 'just knowing the languages and having lived abroad makes you more open to other ways of thinking. It's not so much having the language itself as the knowledge of a different perspective, otherwise you're doing everything from a very anglo-saxon outlook.'

Summary   **Lobbyist**

Role	• To advise their clients/employers on how best to influence the political process to their advantage.
Requirements	*Education*: Degree in any discipline, though politics related may be preferable.
	Nationality: None specified.
	Age limits: None specified – though most Junior and Account Executive posts will go to those in their 20s
	Equal opportunities: Open to all.
	Relevant work experience:Preferable for consultancy, a necessity for in-house.
	Relevant postgraduate qualification: Useful but not required.
Selection Procedure	*Consultancy*: advertisements may appear in *The House Magazine* and specialist recruitment agencies may be

used. But personal contact and speculative application are usual route in. Possibly application form but more usually CV and interview.

In-house: most posts advertised in the quality press and/or relevant professional journals. Recruitment agencies may also be used. CV or application form. Possibly written test on, say, knowledge of political scene, interview(s).

Key Skills and Qualities

• Communication and interpersonal skills; ability to work on own intitiative, under pressure and within a team. Keen interest in politics and understanding of the political process.

Pay and Conditions

Salary, Consultancy: Junior Account Executive, range from £15,000–£20,000, Account Executive up to £23,000 approx, Senior Account Executives up to around £25,000, Account Managers, up to approx. £30,000–£35,000, Directors £40,000 plus.

Salary, In-house varies quite widely £20,000–£30,000.

Hours: Usually 37 hours per week contractual, but flexibility required. Some evening work.

Holidays: Varies 21 days to 30 plus Bank Holidays.

Job Security: Good.

• Political activity is allowed – indeed many lobbyists work voluntarily for the party of their choice, especially at election time.

Further Information

• For lists of consultancies see: *Hollis UK Press and Public Relations Annual* and *Dod's Parliamentary Companion.*

• There are links to various consultancies websites from Politico's resources at www.politicos.co.uk see also Politico's book *Directory of Political Lobbying 2001-2001* by Corinne Souza.

• *The House Magazine* is available from Politico's Bookstore 020 7828 0010.

• For an in-depth look at the techniques of lobbying see *Politico's Guide to Political Lobbying* by Charles Miller.

9   Political parties and trade unions

Political Parties

How often have you watched the TV news reporter standing in front
of the imposing building of Tory Central Office in Smith Square or
the looming tower block of Labour's Millbank talking about the
'party machines'. If you didn't know any better you'd think the
respective parties occupied the whole of those buildings and
employed many hundreds of apparatchiks beavering away, plotting
and spinning. In fact, they occupy only part of those buildings and the
numbers employed are relatively few, and in the smaller parties, even
fewer. Yet, regardless of their size, all parties are the hub of a complex
web of internal relationships between MPs (and other parliamentary
representatives), local councillors, and individual members as well as
being a link to many organisations outside the party political loop
and, of course, the media.

Many of the areas of work covered in this book are influenced by
the political calendar, but few more so than the parties. The emphasis
on certain parts of their work and role, and the numbers of people
doing it, ebb and flow according to the season – the autumn
Conferences and the spring (or in 2001, the summer) general election
with eddies of by-elections, policy forums etc. along the way. But the
most dramatic change is the post general election exodus, at least from
the HQs of the larger parties. Both personnel managers and staff see
party employment as largely cyclical and after the four (or possibly 5)
years of a Government it is accepted that it is time to move on – not
all staff, of course, but a good many. For this reason it is difficult to get
accurate-for-all-time figures on employment. However, to give you
some idea for the main UK-wide parties, the following were accurate
in spring 2000: Conservative Party – 145 staff in London HQ, 85 in
Scotland and Wales Offices plus party agents in the constituencies;
Labour Party – 150 at Millbank and 250 in the 9 regions; Liberal Party

– 40 at the Federal HQ in London, one or two in the England, Scotland and Wales state parties, and one, two or none in the 12 English regions. The regional parties and the Green Party have very small staffs and rely even more heavily on volunteers than the main ones.

As with many of the careers in politics, volunteering can be an invaluable way in to a paid job. However large they are, there isn't a party in the country that has more money than it needs. Reliant as they are on membership dues and possibly merchandise sales, but largely donations, there is never enough cash to employ all the staff they could use. But apart from this practical, and possibly mercenary, reason voluntary activity is a traditional and respected part of the party political world and many see it as a valuable way of allowing more people to become involved. And, the work you do as a volunteer can be varied and interesting – it's not all admin and envelope-stuffing! In the Green Party, for example, people with some research, writing and/or desktop publishing skills can work with the staff research teams on generating policy across a whole range of issues from the economic and environmental impacts of aviation to world trade. In any party you could be involved in media monitoring, setting up databases, fact finding etc. and at general election time it's all hands to the pump.

The 'war rooms' of all the parties at the last election were supplemented with young and not so young volunteers; some with more enthusiasm than experience and others, ex-party workers, lobbyists etc., with a wealth of knowledge. Occasionally there are opportunities for paid work experience – I did come across a gap year student working in the press office at the Liberal Democrat HQ before going on to a degree in History and Politics (she had been active in her local party previously). But whether paid or voluntary, time spent with the party will give you an insight into its internal workings and of the political scene more generally. Even if you can't, or decide you don't want to, get into party work you will have gained knowledge and skills to enhance your CV and very likely have made valuable contacts in other spheres of the political world. But so much for volunteering – who does what and gets paid for it?

The 'staffers': Getting as many of its candidates elected as possible is obviously a major aim of the party, but their work covers much more.

All the parties are organised slightly differently (and often take the opportunity of the post-election exodus to re-organise), and use different department and job titles, but they all cover 5 main areas: policy – research, development and dissemination; media and communications; campaigns and elections; fundraising and administration (i.e., membership, personnel, finance etc.). Of these, the first three are probably more likely to appeal to people with an interest in politics. However, if you already have experience in administration, marketing, personnel etc. and want to work in a political organisation then the opportunities do exist.

Policy: The process by which policy is developed and finally agreed differs between parties but will involve, to a greater or less extent, the elected representatives, their staff and the membership at large. However, the staff at HQs will play a large part in doing the research and development as well as helping to communicate it to all sections of the party network. Claire Healy is the Health Policy Officer at the Labour Party and she explains more. 'Basically there are two main aspects to my role. The first is communication; we communicate to the party what we're doing in government but equally we [policy officers] let those in government know what the party at large is thinking and feeling. That takes the form of daily and weekly briefs that go out to MPs, MEPs and so on. We do briefs around particular issues, also campaigning dossiers, provide information to the Parliamentary Labour Party, and local councillors as well as members. The second aspect of the job is policy development. The party develops its policies over two years via national policy forums. Each policy area has what is called a policy commission which is made up of government members, representatives of the National Executive Committee [Labour Party ruling body] and constituency members. Submissions come in from various parts of the Party and then we put together the draft policy document which, when agreed, forms the basis of the election manifesto.'

Policy officers therefore become very knowledgeable about the areas for which they are responsible, but they also have to be politically aware. For example, as an academic studying health policy you would look dispassionately at both sides of any case and put forward the arguments on either side. Party policy documents, on the other hand, are written from a specific political perspective and therefore some possible solutions to issues or problems cannot be countenanced for political reasons, or at least, they would have to be couched in politically acceptable ways. Whatever party you work for as a policy officer, (also called researcher) you will need to appreciate this and be able to identify with the aims of the organisation. As another policy officer pointed out, you also have to have 'the ability to turn concepts and ideas into political bullet points and campaigns' as well as develop relationships with the groups involved in policy making and 'to understand their concerns and where their bottom line is'. Interpersonal and negotiation skills are paramount.

Policy/research officers are almost always graduates and come from a variety of disciplines. They might also have one or two years experience in other types of political work (for an MP for example) or in a think tank or in something related to a policy specialism. For example, Claire had spent some time on the National Health Service Financial Management Training Scheme. As well as good analytical skills, you will need the ability to write clearly and succinctly, to co-operate with others and work well under pressure. Jobs will be advertised in the quality press, often the *Guardian* and on party websites.

Media and communications: Good communication is vital. Internally all elements of the party organisation need to be kept informed of what's going on in the others and, in the case of the Party in power, the government. If this communication breaks down, it could have ramifications both for efficiency and morale, particularly if segments of the party feel ignored or undervalued. Even more important in public relations and thus electoral terms, is the relationship with the media, national and local.

To a large extent, all staff will be involved in maintaining good internal communications through their day to day activities and dealings with each other. There are often internal magazines for party members and, of course, websites are now a valuable source of information. Handling the media, however, mainly falls to those in the communications sections, and particularly the Press Office. Broadly speaking their role is to monitor what's being said in the media, press and broadcast, about them, their rivals and the issues of the day; to counter any negative stories; to ensure that their Party's view is put across as clearly and as often as possible; to try to spot any potential banana skins before they cause injury; and keep all the spokespeople for the party singing from the same hymn sheet – at least as much as possible! This work goes on throughout the year, but obviously at election times, particularly general elections, the pace is more frenetic and the stakes even higher. Alan Rodger is a Press Research Officer in the Scottish Conservative Office and lived through the 7am to 10pm working days of the 2001 general election. 'There are 6 of us in the section, though during the election some people came in on contract to help out. Throughout the election we were preparing briefs for the spokespeople each day and doing any research that was needed on the particular policies and campaigns. We produced a daily bulletin – The Campaigner – which focussed on the themes of the day and was emailed to all candidates. A lot of the work was responding to calls from journalists who wanted information on the policies or comment on what the other parties were saying or doing, or on anything else that they thought might be newsworthy. The media monitoring – watching the broadcast media, reading all the press coverage etc. – which goes on all the time anyway, is particularly important at elections.'

Of course, press office work is not always as frenetic or the hours as long, but you do have to be able to work under pressure and to come up quickly with responses to what are often complex or awkward questions. You need to understand how the media functions and what is newsworthy which is why many press officers will have come from a background in journalism, public relations or press relations in other organisations. However, it's not impossible to get straight in, as Alan proves. He joined the press office more or less straight from university (degree in Business from Strathclyde) and with a history of local party activism.

Campaigns and Elections: Just about all party staff have to be aware of the need to campaign all year round whether there's an election in the offing or not, and many roles will have an element which keeps them in touch with the issue, for example policy officers producing campaign dossiers for staff. Plus there will always be staff at HQ whose main responsibility is campaign organisation and planning. However, most of the ongoing campaigning goes on at grassroots level out in the regions and the constituencies. Much of this is done by the local party activists, i.e. volunteers, but certainly the Conservative and Labour Parties have a number of full-time paid organisers. In the former, these are the party agents, of whom John Earl was one for nearly 10 years before moving to positions at regional and then Central Office. He joined as a young graduate in 1977 and worked in the East Midlands, Leicester and Loughborough. 'The political agent is almost like the Chief Executive Officer of the local party organisation. In each constituency there is a Conservative Association and in many cases the agent is the only paid employee (plus secretary). You have to do everything basically; you maintain membership records, deal with finance, raise money, build and create new branches, encourage new members and most of all organise and support the volunteers locally. Where there is a Conservative MP you are effectively their local representative and at election time you are more or less the campaign manager and have to know about everything from printing to election law, though you do get training on that. Being a political agent is a 'fix' thing; you don't do it for the money. The hours are long with many of them in the evening when the volunteers are available after their own day's work. It's not a career for the faint-hearted.'

This last sentiment is certainly shared by Kim Andrews-Devine, Labour Party Regional Organiser, North. 'Most organisers are very committed to what they do. It's not just a job. It's demanding mentally and physically – you're asked to do all sorts of things – usually at the drop of a hat, especially during elections. In June [2001 election] I ran the regional print scheme producing all the promotional literature for constituencies in the region that meant numerous leaflets, calling cards, posters and so on as well as co-ordinating the postal votes and other more strategic things including working alongside the visits team organising Ministers' visits to the constituencies in my area. It was very hard work, but the rewards were enormous. We had some amazing events in the region. Tony Blair and John Prescott came and it was wonderful seeing members of the public as well as the party being able to talk to them direct – these are people they'd normally only see on the TV.'

Organisational ability is fundamental for the job, but so are people skills. As an organiser or agent you will assess what needs to be done in the constituency but you will have to rely on the volunteers to make it happen. The ability to get on with very different kinds of people and be able to motivate them are crucial to your success. And it's not easy. They will all have other calls on their time and getting them to be active, particularly for the less enjoyable things like leafleting on a cold, dark, wet evening, will call on all your powers of persuasion. Paid organisers come from a wide range of backgrounds, often arriving via local party activism but from jobs in completely different spheres of working life. However, it is possible for younger people including new graduates to succeed. When John Earl joined in the late 1970s as a new graduate he was very much in a minority, but now more younger people are becoming Conservative Party agents. Kim Andrews–Devine had spent almost 7 years in the Air Force as a linguist before doing a degree in Community and Youth Work and then joining the Labour Party's Trainee Organiser scheme, (though recruitment to this scheme is now suspended). How long people then stay in the job varies greatly. Because of the hours and commitment required, it can put enormous strains on personal and family relationships so some people will move on quite quickly, perhaps to other spheres in the political world.

Apart from these main areas, each party may have other roles peculiar to its own position in the political spectrum, perhaps linking to interested or affiliated external organisations. For example, the Labour Party obviously has very strong links with the Trade Union movement and employ a full-time Trade Union Liaison Officer, Natascha Engel. Twenty three unions, including all the largest ones such as Unison, AEEU, TGWU and GMB, affiliate to the Labour Party and her role, as she describes it, is to 'make sure the affiliated unions play an active role in every aspect and at every level of the Labour Party.' Natascha is based at Millbank and liaises with the General Secretaries, trade union political officers, regional trade union officials and constituency-based trade union liaison officers. There are also ad hoc meetings, usually every couple of months, between the unions' leaders and the Party. Chaired jointly by Tony Blair and Bill Morris (TGWU), topics discussed by the National Trade Union and Labour Party Liaison Committee include both policy and organisation –

especially in the run up to the general election when the focus was exclusively on campaigning.

As well as the national committee, there is another at regional level, where union Regional Secretaries meet with the Regional Labour Party in each of its 11 regions. Here campaigning needs are discussed for by-elections as well as the general, local and European ones. For Natascha this means a lot of travelling up and down the country, but as she says, 'it also means getting to know a lot of people and understanding local issues better. The relationship between the Party and the unions always works best where people have informal relationships, so it's important to make sure that you get people together as often as possible. And nothing is more fun than running campaigns with lots of people – especially general elections.'

Prior to joining the Labour Party, Natascha had just completed her training as a Trade Union organiser, of which more in the next section.

Summary	**Political Party Worker – 1. policy/research; 2. media/communications; 3. organiser/agent**
Role	1. To research and help formulate party policy
	2. To liaise with the media and brief others in the party who may have contact with the media
	3. To organise and support local party activists and campaigns
Requirements	*Education*: None necessarily specified, though 1 and 2 will almost always be graduates
	Nationality: None specified
	Age limit:: None specified
	Equal opportunities: Open to all
	Relevant work experience: May be specified
	Relevant postgrad. qual. Not required
Key Skills and Qualities	1. Research, analytical, negotiation, writing and presentation skills. Political awareness.
	2. Ability to assimilate information, think on your feet and work under pressure
	3. Organisational and interpersonal skills

Selection Procedure	• Vacancies may be advertised in Party magazines/papers/websites, and/or quality national papers, and/or minority publications.
	• Application form or CV. Interview(s) and possibly written tests
Pay and Conditions	• Salaries vary widely. Approximate range depending on seniority from £17,000 to £30,000
	• Other terms and conditions by negotiation
Further Information	See individual party websites

Trade Unions

There are over 200 unions in the UK with a combined membership of 7.8 million. The roll call of their names encompasses almost the whole range of industries and professions and recalls not a little of our history. The Card Setting Machine Tenters Society and the General Union of Loom Overlockers are redolent of our industrial past. Even the full name of ASLEF, the train drivers' union, harks back to its historical roots – The Associated Society of Locomotive Engineers and Firemen. But present day unions are just that – in the present. Collectively, they may not have the same political with a large 'P' power that they had in the 1960s and '70s, but they continue to have influence. As workers' organisations, their primary role, of course, is to support their membership in the workplace, so much of their work is concerned with purely industrial relations matters and training etc. However, workplaces exist in regional and national economies and employment-related issues impact on social and political life.

In terms of employment, many of those who work for their unions do so on a voluntary basis, Shop Stewards and Branch Secretaries for example. The number of paid staff will vary dramatically, often according to the size of the union, in terms of membership, and the type and range of industries covered. For example the GMB which represents workers in an enormous range of industries from security to shipbuilding and is one of the half dozen or so with a membership in excess of three quarters of a million, employs over 500 full and part-time staff. At the other end of the scale is the Ceramic and Allied Trades Union (ceramic industries) has around 21,000 members and employs 16 staff and Equity, the performers' union, has around 35,000 members and 56 staff. Many union staff will be concerned specifically with membership and workplace issues, for example at the Graphical, Paper and Media Union (GPMU) the majority of the 30 staff are involved in vocational training, health and safety matters and advising on legal and equality issues as well as the general administration that any organisation needs. Most of these specialist staff will have come up through the union's unpaid ranks and/or moved in from other spheres with the relevant knowledge and experience behind them. However, there are four areas of work which may be of more interest to readers, namely Research Officers, Political/Parliamentary Officers, Press Officers (which in the larger unions are discrete jobs but in the smaller are often combined) and full-time paid Organisers. To take the last first.

Branch Organisers: Michael Moran is a Branch Organiser at NATFHE (University and College Lecturers Union) and he explains his role: 'On a day-to-day basis I go out to talk to branches about how to improve their organisation, how they communicate with their members. I help them recruit new members and get involved in training new Union representatives. Back in the office, I'll be setting up and maintaining databases on membership and feeding back to the national organisation on policy and recruitment issues.'

Recruiting new members, particularly in organisations or companies that are hostile to the idea of trade union activity or where the workers are traditionally hard to involve, is not an easy task; it requires skill, knowledge, tact and planning. To prepare them for the task, many new organisers have come through the Trades Union Congress (TUC) Organising Academy training scheme. (The TUC is an umbrella body which lobbies and campaigns on behalf of unions and working people in general and also provides various services for its 74 member unions.) On the scheme, trainees have periods at the TUC's education centre but work mainly with experienced staff in individual unions. They learn how to plan a campaign – how to resource it, how to build rapport with contacts in the workplace as well as make alliances in the local community, and how to involve the media. There are about 30 places on the scheme each year and while there is no age limit most of the trainees have been in their mid to late 20s. Nor is there a minimum educational requirement, but at the selection assessment centre they will be looking for commitment, drive, enthusiasm and organising skills. Many successful applicants have a background in trade unionism but others have come from areas such as the women's movement or other social campaigns. The scheme pays £19,000 and lasts a year. A job is not guaranteed at the end of it, but most people do get posts either with the union they've worked with during the year. However, a few people will choose to move to other political or campaigning organisations, as did Natascha Engel who is now with the Labour Party and who featured in the previous section.

Her academic background was in modern languages and after brief spells as a trainee journalist on a local newspaper, teaching abroad and an MA in translation, she spent three and a half years working as a TV sub-titler. It was during this time that she became actively involved in the Labour Party and her trade union. When she saw the advertisement in the *Guardian* for the TUC Organising Academy she went for it and worked with the GPMU, the union for printing and allied trades. 'It was quite a culture shock. The environments I'd worked in before – TV post-production and education – were both very diverse and laid back. The first couple of weeks at the GPMU were a bit of a battle to make sure that some full-time officials realised that I wasn't there to do their typing! But I was lucky to have a coach who was herself a young woman who understood the challenges. And the work was incredibly rewarding. I was basically being paid full-time to do what I'd be doing in my free time anyway.'

'The most memorable and exciting experience was organising our Union Week which we built around the introduction of the Working Time Directive. We got a van and parked outside all the different workplaces where we'd been organising and advertised when we would be there to explain the Directive and give advice on any other matters. On the evening of the last day we had a massive party in Covent Garden. On top of that we recruited loads of new members.'

On the face of it, organising might not seem to be the sort of job of interest to someone wanting to be involved in politics per se, but as Michael Moran points out 'Trade unionism is very much part of a social movement that seeks justice, equality and respect for working people. Modern organising is a return to grassroots trade unionism encouraging a bottom up rather than a top down approach to decision making. Anyway, workplace and political agendas collide in all sorts of ways.'

Research, Political/Parliamentary and Press Officers: As a Research Officer at GMB, Ida Clemo is one of a team of 6 and specialises in the food and leisure industries. Amongst other things her work includes:

- keeping up to date with what's going on in the industries – looking for trends, watching how individual companies are performing and writing briefing notes as required

- helping to write speeches for Officials, doing the background research, providing key points

- responding to calls from government on consultation papers, e.g. on Licensing Law reform

- helping to formulate pay claims, where there are national agreements, and writing bargaining briefs

- answering questions from members and regional officers, some of which may need to be referred on to other specialist departments

In fact Ida and her colleagues in the research team at GMB are in a small minority. It is only in the very big unions that individuals have truly specialist roles like hers. (For another example of a specialist in a large union, please see the chapter on Public Affairs for the case study of Alexa Knight, Parliamentary Officer at the Royal College of Nursing.) Most unions and the TUC regional offices, have modest numbers of staff so one person will often work across the range of the research, political and press functions. Dave Green is the only Research Officer at the National Union of Knitwear, Footwear and Apparel Trades (KFAT) which has around 20,000 members. 'Because we're a small organisation I do a lot more than the usual research stuff. I'm also responsible for all the press and PR and publications. The research involves finding out information for our full-time officials and members. There's also a fair amount of queries on employment law to be answered. We need to respond to consultations from the TUC and the Government. Most recently, the Government is planning changes to the working time regulations and we've been sent circulars from both the TUC and the Department for Trade and Industry. I'll ask our own districts if they've got any views and then I'll feed it back. I'm also the Union's Political Officer as well. That really means liaising with the Labour Party and making sure that the interests of our industry get put across to relevant MPs. We have a list of MPs from areas of the country where textiles are, or at least used to be, a dominant industry and we keep in touch with them through emails and letters – general lobbying. I also edit the Union's journal which comes out three times a year.'

At the Wales TUC, Darron Dupre works as both researcher and press officer. He will write reports commissioned by the General Council of the Wales TUC which may then be part of formal submissions to the Welsh Assembly on anything from the Private Finance Initiative to a manufacturing strategy for Wales, and will sometimes involve meetings with Ministers with the General or Assistant General Secretary. In the past year Darron has also presented evidence (written and verbal) to the National Assembly Subject Committes on behalf of the Wales TUC and led the Call Centre Campaign. The press work is mainly reacting to calls from the local media, often unforunately about job losses such as those at Corus the steel manufacturer. But he is also proactive, writing and issuing press releases and phoning around people in the media to remind them that organisations representing workers are every bit as important as employers' associations.

Finally, Martin Brown at Equity is not only responsible for Press and PR but also Campaigns, though he does have a colleague who works on research and parliamentary affairs. 'I oversee the publication of the Union's journal, and communication with members as well as the annual review and other occasional publications. I handle the majority of the press enquiries and am either involved or oversee all the Union's campaigning activities. Most recently we've been involved in organising a cross–industry conference with government Ministers, employers, theatre directors and performers to discuss issues to do with disability – mainly training and employment. I can't really say how much time I spend on each of the aspects of the job. My days are always a tapestry of interwoven tasks. For example, this morning I'm trying to write the next journal, and I'm doing a press interview in about 10 minutes, then this afternoon I'm involved in talks with film producers as part of our campaign for better pay for actors when they're working in British films.'

Getting In: On the whole, work in trade unions is not usually an option for those straight out of university. Previous trade union activity and/or relevant experience is usually required. So, for example, Ida Clemo had worked in the commercial sector, Dave Green in other unions, Martin Brown in journalism, and Darron Dupre and Natascha Engel had both been active in their union on a voluntary basis whilst in other jobs.

Summary	**Trade Unions, 1. Branch organiser; 2. Research/Parliamentary/Press officer**
Role	1. To support local officials and encourage recruitment 2. To provide research on relevant issues to members and officials/to lobby legislators and others on union's behalf/to liaise with the media
Requirements	*Education*: 1. None specified, 2. Degree may or may not be specified, but most successful applicants will be graduates *Nationality*: None specified *Age limit*: None specified *Equal opps.* Open to all *Relevant work experience*: Usually required and/or previous trade union activity *Postgrad. qualification*: Not required
Selection Procedure	• Posts will be advertised in The Guardian and possibly minority press • For TUC Organising Academy Training Scheme there is an assessment centre, otherwise by interview(s) and possibly written tests
Pay and Conditions	*Salary*: Trainee organiser £19,000 Research/Parliamentary/Press Officer varies greatly.

Range from approximately £18,000 to £29,000

- Other conditions will also vary but usually standard 37 hours per week and 23-28 days holiday plus Bank holidays.

Further Information

- Links to all unions affiliated to the TUC are on that website at www.tuc.org.uk.

Interview   **Greg Rosen**

Though just 4 years into his career Greg Rosen already has experience of working for a political party, in political consultancy, for a Trade Union and for an all-party campaign group

CV

Education	MA History, Edinburgh
	Secondary schooling in London
Career	1997 Labour Party, HQ
	1997–9 Public Policy Unit, (political consultancy)
	1999– AEEU, Research Officer and on secondment to Britain in Europe

What was your first job?

When I graduated in 1997, I worked for a few months at Labour Party Headquarters in the Attack and Rebuttal Unit. I'd been helping out informally and then I was offered the job. Unfortunately, after the election the organisation was being reviewed and the unit I was in was radically downsized. The structure that was decided on did not have roles for those of us who had been working in that unit so we all moved on.

Moved on to what?

I joined the Public Policy Unit [a public affairs consultancy] *as a Political Consultant working in a number of areas. Most of my colleagues were retired civil servants who had a considerable degree of expertise and knowledge of government but less of a feel for the contemporary political scene. I was working with clients ranging from a county council and Rail Link Engineering (the Channel Tunnel rail link) to the Heritage Lottery Fund and New Opportunities Fund. I was involved in giving them strategic political advice, community relations, devising communications strategies and advising them on how to put a case. Basically, however well you put a bad case it will still be a bad case: if a boat won't hold water it doesn't matter how nicely you paint it, it will still sink. On the other hand, if you have a decent case you can still put it badly: you can make a perfectly seaworthy boat unattractive by painting it the wrong colour.*

I was there for about a year and half and then it was bought out by Citigate, but I had decided to move on anyway. It was an education. But I'm in politics to work for what I believe in and as a consultant you can't choose your clients. So in 1999 when I saw the advertisement for the post of Research Officer with the AEEU, I applied and got it.

And what did that work involve?

Very soon after I joined, I was offered the opportunity of a secondment to Britain in Europe as Policy and Research Officer. Initially we were setting up the organisation. Because we were a small team, everyone had to get involved in every aspect. I wrote one of the pamphlets and drafted letters, articles and briefings, but I was doing all sorts of other things – political liaison and media work, explaining to potential supporters in business and politics who we were and what we were doing. It was a complete variety of things and a very exciting time. Britain in Europe is an historic coalition. When we launched there had never been an occasion in recent British politics when the Prime Minister and Chancellor of the Exchequer sat side by side with politicians who in all other circumstances would be seen as their political adversaries.

After the launch the staff did go more into their respective niches. Basically I was producing briefings across a range of issues – often rebutting the myths about Europe – for the media and the organisation's supporters.

Then a few weeks ago in February I was temporarily brought back to the Union as a Press Officer. We are in the midst of a ballot to merge with the MSF union that would create a new super union with over one million members in every sector of the UK economy. The new union would be the biggest affiliate to the Labour Party, the second biggest in the TUC and the biggest in companies like BAE Systems, Rolls Royce, Siemens, Jaguar, Vauxhall, Glaxo, Marconi Communications and Royal and Sun Alliance. It is a very exciting time and a historic opportunity for Britain's trade-union movement. In addition to the media relations role I am also covering a couple of the Union's industries – producing briefings, for example, for union negotiators. It is keeping me pretty busy.

What would you say are the main skills or qualities needed in the type of work you've done?

You need to be a team player, to enjoy working with people in general and be able to communicate effectively. You need to be able to understand how organisations work and interpret the political context in which you're working, for example, things need to be written in different ways for different audiences.

The key thing I would say is that politics isn't just a job, it is the forum in which we all decide how we're governed. It involves belief, ideals and a lot of hard work and hopefully in the end, results in terms of a better society. It's not a nine to five thing; if you believe in what you are doing you don't just switch off at 5 o'clock.

I think one of the best textbooks about politics is by John P. Mackintosh, The Government and Politics of Britain. *The reason it's so good is because he was an MP as well as an academic and had a real feel for what he was writing about. Having said that, you can read as many books as you can fit on your shelves, but you won't get a proper feel for what the structures and diagrams mean in practice unless you've actually been part of it.*

The best way to get a job in politics is to get involved in it. That's how you get the skills and experience that make you employable. It's also important to keep your feet on the ground. Remember that you are part of a greater whole. The way to get over the Catch 22 of no job without experience and no experience without a job, is to get involved on a voluntary basis. At university I was Secretary of the Labour Club,

Vice-Chair of the Scottish Young Fabians, re-founded the Edinburgh University Fabian Society and got involved with campaigning, organising, and helping out at constituency level. Everyone's got spare time and anyone can get involved with their local constituency party or trade union.

10   Journalism

The media dominate our world. In an incredible feat of planning, logistics and teamwork the national newspapers, TV and radio bring us news from around the world – great events at home and far away – on an hourly basis. Is it any wonder then that so many people interested in politics and current affairs dream of being journalists?

But to achieve that dream you have to be dedicated and persistent. What marks out the serious contenders from the armchair wannabees is proof of your commitment – and you need to start collecting trophies on your CV as early as possible.

Julie Peacock is now a trainee at Radio Stoke but she had known from her school days that journalism was her goal and planned accordingly.

'At school I did the school newspaper and I chose my degree, English and International Relations (Aberdeen), with journalism in mind. When I was at university I got involved in hospital radio and ended up doing newsreading and some presenting. During the vacations I worked in a press office, independent production companies and the BBC to get different kinds of work experience.'

And it has ever been thus. Patrick Burns is now Political Editor, BBC Midlands, and was at university in the 1970s (History and Politics at Manchester), but while a student he wrote for the Student Union and Hall of Residence magazines, got involved in student television and did unpaid work experience at a commercial radio station in Birmingham. He also contributed to newspapers whenever he could:

One of the aspects of the course I was studying was the part played by the Roman Catholic Church in Spanish politics and I saw an article in the Birmingham Post *about the role of a Jesuit political pressure group in Spain which I disagreed with. So I wrote a long letter to the* Post *rebutting some of the points in the article. It was published as the lead letter. I would definitely advise anyone who's interested in journalism generally, and political journalism in particular, to use any opportunities at student level of get published. That letter in the* Birmingham Post *was a very useful addition to my scrapbook, because it showed I could engage in grown-up political debate rather than just student politics.'*

Getting work experience in newspapers, radio and TV stations, independent production companies etc. can be difficult. You must be prepared to hassle a bit. Persevere. Use any contacts you may have, write direct to producers, directors and editors rather than personnel departments and literally knock on doors. Students with a disability may find it particularly hard, but the organisation Workable may be able to help (website address in Further Information). Remember that any media experience is valuable. Even if you want to go into TV or radio a stint in the press is useful and vice versa. During your later career you might well move from one to the other anyway. Andrew Marr, the BBC's political editor, for example, moved from press to broadcasting.

As well as directly related work experience, it can be useful to have other 'interesting' things on your CV. Travel and work abroad are good indicators of someone who is independent and interested in different people and places; after her degree, Julie Peacock spent a year teaching English in Japan for example. If your ultimate aim is political journalism then think about work experience in some of the areas covered in this book, or, if you can afford it, perhaps an internship in Washington or a stage in Brussels.

What next?: Armed with your degree (and most of the journalists I spoke to said that politics, history, international relations etc. were better backgrounds to come from than media studies) and work experience, you will then be in a good position to compete successfully for places on the various courses and training schemes at local, or even if you're very lucky, national level. Many of the national broadsheet and tabloid newspapers have graduate training schemes in one guise or another, though there is never a guarantee of a job at the end, they don't necessarily run every year, and altogether they take probably less than 15 people. But for example, the *Mirror* group take on 2 trainees in January and September for 3-year stints at salaries of

£14,000 in the first year, £16,000 in the second and rising to £20,000 in the third. Trainees work on all three papers, *Mirror, Sunday Mirror* and *The People* and in the regional offices in Glasgow, Belfast and Cardiff. Again, the *Sun* takes on a couple of people a year. In the first year trainees do the Postgraduate course in journalism at City University and work on the paper during the vacations, and in the second year are sent on placement to Glasgow and Manchester and either New York or Sydney. Pay is £12,500 plus living expenses. And the *Guardian*, via the Scott Trust Bursary Scheme, supports four students through the journalism courses either at City University or University of Central Lancashire by paying their fees and giving a £4,000 grant. They also give work experience at the *Observer* as well as the *Guardian*. News agencies may also take on trainees and the Press Association runs a three-year News Traineeship Programme with placements in Parliament as well as their regional offices.

Over the past couple of years, the BBC have also supported 8 to 10 students on journalism courses through their News Sponsorship Scheme. They pay course fees and give a grant of £3,5000 plus offering a month's work experience at £230 per week on successful completion of the course. In addition, the BBC also have their Broadcast Journalist Trainee Scheme for regional reporters. This is a one-year scheme, again with no guarantee of a job at the end, but excellent on- and off-the-job training in one of the Beeb's 14 regional newsrooms. The salary is £16,500 plus £2,750 London weighting allowance. This list of schemes is not exhaustive and they will change from year to year, so do check on organisations' websites for up to date details, including closing dates.

With so few places available on the schemes mentioned above, the majority of people will pay for themselves to go through one of the postgraduate journalism courses on offer at colleges and universities up and down the country. A postgraduate qualification is not a require-ment, but because of supply and demand, it can greatly boost your chances of success. Lists of these courses can be found on the websites given in the Further Information section. The other option is to bypass the postgraduate courses and try to get taken on as a permanent employee, starting as trainee, with a local newspaper, radio or TV station immediately following your degree. Many regional media outlets prefer to employ people who know the area, so your own local papers or stations are good starting points.

What are recruiters looking for?: Whether it's a course, a training scheme or a job in the press or broadcast media, all selectors will be looking for similar skills and qualities. You may think that research and writing skills would be top of their agenda. And, yes, of course they want people who can find their way round information, understand what is newsworthy and put together a grammatical piece of writing. But in connection with political and hard news journalism, the words most frequently used to me were – curious, inquisitive, questioning, independent-minded, awkward even. Chris Frost is Senior Lecturer in Journalism at the University of Central Lancashire: 'I'm always staggered at how few people are inquisitive. I've just written a book on reporting and that's how I start the introduction – you've got to be fascinated by people and events. I wouldn't really recommend coming in to journalism because you want to write. I know that may sound a bit strange but journalism is about much more than just writing, it's about telling the truth.' For most serious journalists it is about finding the truth, and this is applies at all levels, even local. Paul Durrant is the News Editor at the *Eastern Daily Press* in Norwich and for him the satisfaction of journalism is simple: 'It's the right to tell somebody something that somebody else would prefer them not to know. Our job is to challenge. To prove. It's to be a watchdog and to de-bunk authority. If there's somebody out there who prefers you not to know about something then it's my job to do my damnedest to make sure you do know. And that's the buzz.' In that sense all serious journalists are investigative journalists, and none more so than the select band of British political correspondents.

The Lobby

The Parliamentary Press Gallery is the umbrella group of all the journalists authorised to work in the House of Commons i.e., those who report the debates, the sketch writers and the lobby correspondents from print, broadcast, national and regional media. All members of the Press Gallery have office space (though not always much of it) at Westminster and many are based there permanently, returning only rarely to the HQs of their media organisations. And all of them are permitted to sit in the gallery reserved for the press and the *Hansard* writers in the Commons' Chamber. What differentiates lobby. i.e. political correspondents, (collectively called 'the Lobby'), from the debate reporters and sketch writers is the fact that they alone are allowed into the Members' Lobby next to the debating chamber in the House – hence the name, of course. What this means in practice is that they have privileged access to MPs.

There are around 260 members of the Press Gallery, and most of them are now members of the Lobby, but it was not always so. John Deans of the *Daily Mail* and Hon. Secretary of the Press Gallery came to the House as a member of *The Times'* reporting team in 1968 when it consisted of just two lobby and twelve debate reporters. Far more column inches were given to straight reporting of debates in the House. At that time the cadre of Lobby Men (and just one woman – Nora Beloff of the *Observer*) was a select group indeed and while the general tenor of political reporting may have been more deferential in those days, the basic ground rules known as 'Lobby Terms' are more or less the same now as then.

Basically there are three types of communication between MP and lobby correspondent: 1. strictly off the record, i.e. anything said can provide background but not be quoted; 2. unattributable – which means it can be quoted but only attributed in a non-specific way, for example 'a senior source close to the Prime Minister said today...'; 3. on the record, where named quotes are allowed. The most ambiguity exists between the first two – off the record and unattributable briefings – either through misunderstanding or, dare I say, in some cases, deliberate misunderstanding. Journalists must decide for themselves where they want to draw the line. Patrick Burns, Political Editor for BBC Midlands, cites a case in point. 'Under the previous government I was talking to a eurosceptic Conservative MP. We both understood that he was speaking to me on Lobby terms and he hinted that the suspension of a number of eurosceptic MPs was on the cards. The conversation was edging toward the question of geography as half of the rebels over Europe were from the West Midlands. I had to say to him that if he actually confirmed the suspension of MPs in my area, he would be straining, probably to breaking point, my ability to continue under Lobby terms. He held back from delivering the next sentence.' However, while Patrick Burns couldn't quote the MP directly, the knowledge that he'd gained from the conversation could inform his reporting of the situation generally and give him leads to follow up with other sources.

The role of the lobby correspondent: So lobby correspondents have privileged access to MPs and work within agreed guidelines, but how do practitioners see their role?

Michael White, Political Editor of the *Guardian*: *A lobby correspondent does not simply sit in the press gallery and write down what MPs and Ministers say in public, they track down news and gossip in all forms. Essentially he/she is a political reporter looking for news from MPs, official reports, think tanks, backbench gossip, party HQ, Ministerial press releases, No. 10 briefings, select committee reports, rows, feuds, TV programmes...24 hours a day.*

Trevor Kavanagh, Political Editor of the *Sun*: *We're here to make use of our privileged access, to keep in touch with politicians and civil servants and spread our net as wide as possible in Whitehall and Westminster. They provide you with what they want you to think the story is and it's the job of the lobby correspondent to find out more, to find out what's behind it. Quite frequently they are not giving you the full story so we probe a bit further and talk to people who know a little more, that's where the lobby access is so valuable. I think our job is to be healthily sceptical about everything we're told, whether it's from the Government or the Opposition.*

Rachel Ward, GMTV: *It's about trying to make politics accessible to people who aren't necessarily interested in it. Politics has an image of lots of middle-aged men in suits who are slightly pompous and who live in a world different from normal people, but it's so important, it affects all our lives. What I try and do is talk about politics in the way that I would do in the pub and bring it to normal people living normal lives.*

Kristiina Cooper, Correspondent for a number of regional papers: *I see our role as really getting under the surface of government and politics. It's to find out what people are really saying about each other and about policy. I've got 30 MPs in my area and my job is to get to know them and under-*

stand their politics and, obviously, get stories. MPs need the regional press to show their voters all the wonderful things they're doing in Westminster and conversely I can produce stories from MPs because I've got good relationships with them. But it is also a form of accountability – if politicians do very little then that can be reflected in the coverage in the newspaper.

There are thus a number of strands to the job – getting beyond the spin and behind the information supplied to find out what's really going on; presenting stories in a way that makes them intelligible and accessible to the general public; and, finally, an element of holding politicians to account. Needless to say, the people on the other side of the fence don't always share the lobby correspondents' view of the world. Politicians complain publicly about political journalists' obsession with the tittle-tattle of Westminster – the who's in and who's out. They say that the real issues are being lost amongst the trivia. In Michael Cockerell's TV documentary, *News From Number 10* (broadcast 15.7.00), Alastair Campbell, the Prime Minister's Press Secretary, says that his role is to get the Government message across to the public but that '...the political press often, not always, but often, are the barrier to that...' He claims that journalists are the real spin doctors and that '...the blurring of news and comment is such now that most news stories are a form of comment.' But the battle lines over the news agenda are not as clear-cut as journalists v. politicians. Away from the hostilities, both sides appreciate the complexity of the relationship between media and politics and understand that whilst each has its own needs, they also need each other – that's what makes it so fascinating. But, to return to the day-to-day realities of working as a political correspondent.

As in any branch of journalism, it's not all action and excitement. Many a cold, wet hour will be spent standing in the wind tunnel that is Downing Street, or on long journeys trailing a Minister or the Prime Minister. And it's hard work. The Commons does not work nine to five so the hours can be long and unsociable, even more so if, like Rachel Ward of GMTV, your deadlines are in the morning. 'If I'm doing live then I get up about 3.30 am, get in the office at 4 am. My first live on air is generally about 6.00 am so I have two hours in which to read the wires [information via the press agencies] talk to people in the office and decide what we think the lines are. After 8 am it's kind of up to me, so I may go home to sleep in the afternoon, but at night I'm usually in bed by 10, unless a story breaks. I worked an 18-hour day when Peter Mandelson resigned – exhausting. But when I don't do live, I'll usually have quite a dossy day and hang round the House of Commons.'

'Hanging round the Commons' is not a trivial pursuit. Maintaining networks of contacts is crucial for a political correspondent. General reporters need the ability to go into new situations every day and make relationships quickly in order to get the co-operation and information they need. As soon as the story has been covered they leave and in most cases will never again see the people they've just met. The very nature of the work of a lobby correspondent, however, involves nurturing longer-term relationships in order to gain and keep the co-operation of the people who can provide information.

The socialising which is frequently the context for exchanging information as well as maintaining contacts, will often take place in the evening in the restaurants and bars in and around the House. This, together with the rather strange hours kept by the House anyway, can get in the way of family life and some women correspondents have chosen to leave, or at least take a break from, their jobs in order to have more time with their children. Despite this, there are more women moving into the Lobby and while tokenism still exists, hopefully it will get less as the culture and working practices gradually change, both within the Gallery itself and in the House in general.

Who are the lobby correspondents? Who they are not, is young, cub reporters. The age of entry might have come down, but you still need to have a few years journalistic experience under your belt before you stand the chance of a job. Members of the older generation of correspondents will have worked their way up through the ranks of regional media and may or may not have degrees. Today's entrants will all have degrees and have honed their journalistic skills through experience and, often, a vocational course.

At 29, Rachel Ward of GMTV is one of the younger ones but she had been working towards it for a number of years. Whilst studying for her degree in English at Oxford she got involved in student radio as well as student politics. In her final year, having decided to go into journalism and with a place on the postgraduate diploma in journalism at City University secured, her Oxford tutor told her about a few weeks unpaid work experience available on a TV programme called *A Week In Politics*. It went well and she was offered a job to start after her course at City. She stayed with the programme until 1997 when, following another few weeks work experience at Channel 4 News, she joined the programme on a series of short-term contracts. Her final job there was as political producer for Elinor Goodman, the political editor. As Rachel explains the producer is a fixer: 'Say Elinor's doing a 6-minute package and there are 4 politicians she needs to interview, I might do that. I'll help her put the pictures together, write the bit that Jon Snow [the main presenter] reads, write facts and figures for graphics – be there for anything she needs'. By now Rachel knew she wanted to be a political correspondent and following a short stay at Sky Television she heard through the grapevine about the job at GMTV and applied.

A regional paper may employ their own political correspondent or they may use an agency called Central Press who have 3 experienced journalists in the House. But the larger newspaper groups will often have a small team of correspondents to feed articles into a number of their titles. Kristiina Cooper works for Northcliffe Newspapers and writes for the *Nottingham Post*, *Leicester Mercury* and *Lincolnshire Echo*, though she is based permanently in London. Like Rachel, Kristiina's degree was also in English, from Birmingham, and she also did the journalism course at City University, but then she abandoned her journalistic ambitions temporarily and worked at Hansard for three years. The following four years were spent working on weekly papers in Berkshire and Coventry before she spotted the job with Northcliffe which married her experience beautifully.

Whatever their educational and work backgrounds, all political correspondents have one thing in common – they're passionate about politics.

It's an exciting place to be. You do feel like you're in the middle of things. It's just an ongoing, fantastic story, there's lots of conflict and ideology – it's all about the battle of ideas and that's what fascinates me.
Kristiina Cooper

I think working as a journalist is the greatest job in the world, it's only topped by being a political journalist in the House of Commons.
Trevor Kavanagh.

What does it take to be a successful journalist?

Undiminished curiosity but also commitment seem to be key; and hard choices may have to be made. The hours are often long and the absences from home, for example of the foreign correspondent, can cause problems with personal relationships. The main way for regional reporters to make the transition to the national papers is to work for them on a casual basis during days off from their local employer (called doing shifts). But as Paul Durrant recalls you have to decide on your own priorities' 'I did shifts on the *Sun* for 3 or 4 years and a few months with the *Mail,* but I was married and then babies came along and your days off get more precious. I had a choice.' Paul chose to stay in the regions which in itself can be a very satisfying career, but if you want to make it on the national stage there will probably have to be personal sacrifices along the way.

One of the more common stereotypes is that to be a successful journalist you have to be hard as nails and twice as pushy. This is a difficult one to answer, because how hard is hard and how pushy is pushy; people will draw the lines in different places. If you want to get to the truth you will need to be sure enough of yourself to do some tough questioning of often powerful people. To get the scoops that are the feather in the cap of all journalists, you will need to compete with fellow reporters (and there are stories about disabling competitors' cars or equipment – God forbid!), but there is also tremendous camaraderie. If you're a political journalist you are less likely to be forced into the door-stepping of ordinary members of the public, but you may, on occasion, help to ruin a political career or two.

Summary   **Journalist**

Role   • To investigate, report, explain and comment on
                              current events and issues

Requirements	*Education*: Min. qualification is 'A' levels, but majority of entrants have degree in any discipline
	Nationality: None specified
	Age limits: Not usually specified but could be some problems for mature entrants
	Equal opportunities: In theory open to all, though some disabilities may be problematic, but see Further Information below
	Relevant work experience:Proof of commitment via work experience or extra-curricular activities is required
	Relevant postgrad. qualif. Not an absolute necessity, but many new entrants will have taken a postgrad. diploma in journalism
Selection Procedure	• Vacancies on training schemes and for trainee journalist jobs will be advertised on the companies own websites and/or in their papers. Speculative application for jobs can be appropriate.
	• CV or application form. Followed usually by written tests including any of a general knowledge and/or local knowledge quiz; writing a brief article from information given; spelling and grammar tests. Plus interview(s)
Key skills and qualities	• Curiosity, determination, commitment, flexibility, communication skills
Pay and Conditions	*Salary*:Varies widely. Trainees can earn anything between £12,000 and £20,000
	Hours, holidays etc.: By negotiation
	Job Security:Varies, in some organisations fixed-term contracts are the norm

Further Information

- The National Council for the Training of Journalists (NCTJ) at www.nctj.org.uk and The Broadcast Journalism Training council at www.bjtc.org.uk both have useful careers information.
- Postgraduate journalism courses are listed on www.prospects.ac.uk
- The publisher Focal Press produce many handbooks (mainly for

those on journalism courses) which make interesting reading about the techniques of press and broadcast journalists

- Autobiographical books by journalists give a very good insight into the work and lifestyle. Some names that spring to mind are Michael Brunson, John Simpson and Martin Bell
- The *Penguin Book of Journalism: Secrets of the Press*. (1999) Edited by Stephen Glover, this is a fascinating series of essays by journalists from all parts of the press
- For those with a disability see www.workableuk.org and www.radar.org.uk for help with finding work experience and possible funding for courses respectively

Interview **Martin Bell OBE**

Martin Bell is equally famous for being a BBC war reporter and the white-suited independent Member of Parliament for Tatton until he stood down in 2001. This interview took place in 2000.

CV

Educated	King's College Cambridge
Career at the BBC	1965–77 TV News Reporter
	1977–8 Diplomatic Correspondent
	1978–89 Chief Washington Correspondent
	1989–93 Berlin Correspondent;
	1993–4 East European Correspondent
	1994–6 Foreign Affairs Correspondent
	1997 Special Correspondent *9 O'clock News*
From 1997–2001	Independent MP for Tatton

How did you get into war reporting?

I was originally a general reporter when television news was at Alexandra Palace; this was way back in 1964. I was just on the taxi rank doing small robberies and crime, the general news of the day. Then I was the guy nearest the door when war broke out. I went and covered Vietnam in 1967 and that Arab Israeli war, and the beginning of the war in Nigeria. Then after a while, if you don't disgrace yourself, if you don't get scooped, if you work hard and if you don't shout at the foreign editor, you do more and more of this and then you become their first choice. And then you find you're not being asked to do anything else at all. The same thing happened to Kate Adie.

Even if you asked to do something else?

Well, I took whatever came. I didn't mind, except towards the end. I was moved into this position without realising it. I mean it was a fascinating job, but rather difficult to survive. When I was in Washington, you did the whole range of things, political reporting, election campaigns, nip down to Nicaragua or El Salvador for small wars. It only became acute when I worked in Berlin and then what happened was the Iraqis invaded Kuwait; that took up six months of my time. After that, almost immediately the war in Yugoslavia started to break out and I did almost nothing else for virtually all that time until my resignation in '97.

Were there conflicts between what you wanted to do and what your editors wanted?

There were the inevitable conflicts which can't be avoided. There were conflicts about whether or not they would take the stories I was offering; journalists think they're on the most exciting story in the world then there would be some royal scandal and the editors wouldn't want to know. Well that happens, that's just human nature. I had conflicts about the length. I would want longer than they would give me, that's natural, happens all the time. We had a lot of arguments on issues of good taste and the portrayal of real life violence. They were insisting on censorship or self-censorship so acute I felt we were falsifying the picture. We were showing war as an acceptable way to resolve problems. So that was a matter of morality. We argued about this until I left. If I were still in the BBC I would still be arguing about I'm sure.

So, if the opportunity of becoming an MP hadn't come up, would you have stayed with the BBC?

It was never a resignation matter because I always believe in fighting one's corner from inside. But at the time I left the BBC I was only a year and a quarter from being retired, I was up against the 60th birthday.

Do you agree that journalists need to be members of the 'awkward squad'?

I think that's true. Certainly war reporting tends to attract non-conformists, or maybe it's the other way round. The non-conformists in an organisation are sent out to distant war zones where their natural aggression and mischief making can be put to good use.

Are you naturally aggressive?

I was a very shy young man, but I was as aggressive as it was necessary to become. But I was more co-operative than most journalists, even to an extent with my rivals. I didn't have the attitude that many have – it is not enough that I must win, but you must lose.

Who should never go into journalism?

Somebody for whom it would be merely a way of earning a living. Somebody of less than the usual level of concentration. Somebody who would like to work regular and predictable hours. Someone who would like to guarantee a stable, family life. But I'm talking there about travelling journalism. I'm sure you could work for the Angling Times and have a very satisfying family life.

Do you think the growth of online journalism is changing the skills that people need?

The basic skills are the same. I don't think they differ so much medium to medium. Obviously you need the ability to write. There are people who can write for newspapers who can never make the transition to television. It can be difficult the other way round too. But obviously you develop particular skills for whatever field you're in. The qualities you need for war reporting are an insatiable curiosity, a measure of courage and steadiness under fire and a certain amount of moral commitment; it's not just another way of earning a living. If you just want a way of earning a living you should keep bees or do accountancy or something like that.

If you were talking to someone going into journalism now what would you say to them?

Well, if you're talking about war reporting I would tell them it's exceptionally dangerous and I would probably advise against it on those grounds.

If you're not a casualty, your family life will be. I don't know which of my 3 wives you'd like to interview about that! And it has become very competitive, very tough, so many agencies and networks competing to get at the same battlefield. You know when the intervention in Kosovo happened NATO troops were accompanied or followed by 3000 journalists. It's mad, absolutely mad.

So when did you decide to choose politics over journalism and become an MP?

Well I didn't choose it as much as it chose me. I wasn't looking for it. I assure you I didn't initiate anything. They came looking - the two opposition parties at the time — and I wasn't their first choice. They needed somebody who was known and non-political. I was their second choice; their first choice was Terry Waite who comes from the constituency.

I'd opened an exhibition of Bosnian war photographs at the South Bank Centre taken by Tom Stoddart who was at the Sunday Times *then, and wounded at about the same time I was, though his was much worse. He fell over under fire and broke his ankle and his shoulder and was out of action for a year. His partner in life was Kate Hoey who is now the Sports Minister. At dinner after I'd opened the exhibition, she looked at me and said you're what we want and they explained the circumstances. Instead of telling them to get lost, I really thought it was just dinner table chat, I said call me tomorrow. The next day I got a call from Alastair Campbell and Paddy Ashdown sounding me out about my politics. It took off from that, so I decided very fast. And I thought, let's go for it. I don't like having regrets. At least all the regrets I have tend to be about the things I've not done and wished I had.*

Have you found it as fulfilling as you thought it would be?

I had no idea what it would be like. I knew it would be hard work. And it is very hard work, in London and the constituency. It's more difficult for me because I don't have a party and can't take formal advice from anyone. But then it's also easier for me because I don't have a party. I don't have a whip telling me what to do. I wasn't up last night for an all-night sitting, my chief whip sent me home at half past ten! I like being in a position to vote on every issue on what I perceive to be its merits, it's a wonderful privilege. Not a lot of MPs have got a choice.

What about the constituency work, do you enjoy that?

Yes. I find the tedium is in the chamber. You know, I thought I'd love sitting in the chamber making occasional speeches, and that I'd find the constituency work less fulfilling, but it's actually the other way round. The constituency has to do with kids, with schools, it's great. Not in all cases, but in some, you can actually see results.

A Liberal Democrat MP was attacked at a surgery recently, do you worry about that?

I get a bigger mailbag than most MPs. I can tell just by looking at the size of my mountain of mail when the full moon is. I mean really. One period of time in a month, the amount of green ink mail just rises. But no, it's a much safer job than my last one! I got one death threat last year, that's all.

And is it hard work?

You do a lot of driving, go to a lot of receptions and, especially in the constituency, you're never really off duty. You're a kind of a public figure, you just have to behave in a certain way. I have to be especially careful. The Sun would love to have me on its front page — three in a bed, or something.

What do you think of the media now you're on the other side of the fence?

I find them easier to deal with, having been part of it. I know what they want; I know how to make soundbites. I know that if you've got anything that's bothersome you get it out, you don't go for death by a thousand cuts. No, it's useful. They're entitled to go for me, they did in my campaign but they didn't find anything damaging. But often I ask myself what are they going to find out that I've forgotten.

How do the tabloid journalists differ from the broadsheets?

Well if the tabloids call me it'll only be one of those celebrity round ups, what do you think about whatever the issue of the day is. The Daily Mirror *went for me after 9 months because somebody told them I hadn't declared that my legal fees were paid for by the two parties that stood their candidates down. So, I just paid it out of my savings. That was an awkward 48 hours. But I asked my constituents if they thought I had done anything wrong, 7 said I had and 700 said I hadn't and I soldiered on.*

Do you get much criticism?

No, I get very little negative coverage. Most MPs will be attacked in their constituency by their political opponents. I don't really have political opponents. The Conservatives are especially gracious. They've selected their candidate and we have lunch sometimes and talk about things. The constituency has taken a 4-year holiday from the clamour of party politics and I think they rather like it.

Martin Bell has written two autobiographical books on his experiences as a war reporter and an MP: *In Harm's Way* (1996) and *An Accidental MP* (2000).

11 And a few more

Market research – political polling

Market research is used by organisations of all kinds to evaluate their performance and inform their planning and decision-making. And it's big business; a figure quoted on the Market Research website puts it at £1 billion. Although political polling accounts for just a small portion of this, its capacity to grab headlines, especially at election time, belies its small share of the business.

Most of us will have been approached by market research companies at some time or other via questionnaire mailshots, accostings in the street by their interviewers with clip boards or maybe we've agreed to a longer individual and group interview. 'When did you last buy this? Have you heard of this or that company or product? Do you read this newspaper/magazine more than once a week?' Or for political polls: 'how did you vote at the last election? How do you intend to vote next time? How would you rate the Government's handling of such and such an issue?' The questions may be simple and straightforward but their planning is part of a complex process to ensure that the data collected, plus its analysis and presentation, give the truest representation of people's attitudes or behaviour in relation to the product or issue being investigated.

It is the role of the Market Research Executives to devise and organise the data collection and then interpret the results. Of course it involves number-crunching in the form of sophisticated statistical analysis, but it also requires in-depth knowledge of research methodologies and the psychology of questionnaire design and group dynamics; organisational skills to run the whole project; the ability to present the findings appropriately and, not least, the commercial awareness and interpersonal skills needed to liaise effectively with clients.

Three of the market research companies best known in the context of political polling are NOP, MORI and Gallup. In all of them the number of staff employed in the political research sections is small, usually in single figures, though staff from other sections may be drafted in when business is brisk, during elections for example. Equally, staff in political research sections may often do commercial work and the graduate training schemes usually involve work in all the sections, so anyone considering this area of work must be interested in market research in general, not just political polling. NOP for example recruit about 12–15 graduates a year to the company as a whole and are moved between sections. Individuals interested in political work can only join that section when vacancies occur. Similarly MORI's graduate training scheme which recruits about 16 people during a year encourages staff to spend time in different teams.

Both MORI and NOP accept graduates of any discipline, though they do want to see evidence of research methods training and a MSc in Research/Survey Methods is an advantage.

Gallup on the other hand tends to recruit to specific positions as and when they need people. Simon Sarkar joined the company in October 2000 and whilst he does some commercial work, he is responsible for political polling. His degree was in politics from Essex University (1995), but he also has a MSc in Marketing from UMIST (University of Manchester Institute of Science and Technology) which involved a 6-month research project, as well as work experience in public sector financial management and marketing. So as he says, 'political work is a kind of marriage of my academic background of politics, marketing and market research'. Being an international organisation, there are some opportunities for overseas postings and Simon was sent out to Princeton USA to work on the last American election: 'It was a very exciting place to be and a really good opportunity to see how it's done over there. In fact, a lot of the training at Gallup is done in the States.'

As well as market research, Gallup are involved in consultancy for recruitment and their own recruitment procedure is rigorous. Simon had to go through an online application programme – Strength Finder – which is designed to do just that, i.e. find the strengths within the individual and see whether they are suited to the role on offer. There were then 2 telephone interviews and, on one day, three face to face interviews with different members of the company.

Companies will advertise their graduate schemes and other vacancies on their websites and Gallup uses a variety of sources including the *Guardian* and the *Prospects* publications available from university careers services. Starting salaries for graduates range from about £16,500 up to £18,500, though slightly more experienced entrants can expect £20,000 plus various performance related payments.

Local Government and Quangos

Although there are local authorities up and down the country, the employment for new graduates outside of specialist areas such as town planning, environmental health etc., are extremely limited. Councils work on tight budgets and, as it was described to me, 'local authorities tend to like their graduates job-ready.' It is often people from the voluntary, education or private sectors who have the right mix of knowledge and experience for roles such as Policy Officer, European Officer, Regeneration Officer, Research and Information Officer or Press and Parliamentary Officer. The other areas covered in this book could well provide the necessary background for these roles. Or, graduates will move within the local authority sector from one specialism to another or by starting in a fairly lowly administrative position and working their way up. Having said that, there is now a work placement scheme offering penultimate year students 5-weeks paid experience in the summer. Some of the placements on offer on the scheme may be applicable to those with an interest in politics. For more information on this and other career-related issues see the Local Government National Training Organisation website at www.lgnto.org.uk. In general, the advice for those wanting to work in local government is to get the relevant experience in another sphere and move across a couple of years down the line.

The same advice applies to quangos (quasi non-governmental organisations also called non-departmental government bodies). You can find a full list of the 1000 or so of these organisations at the Cabinet Office website www. cabinet-office.gov.uk. They range in function from specialist advisory bodies on genetics or whatever, to museum trusts to the Millennium Commission. Most have very small permanent staffs, mainly concerned with administration. Any specialist posts of possible interest to readers will require relevant experience acquired elsewhere.

Academic Publishing

Having spent much of your life to date reading textbooks and other serious works about subjects that interest you, you may be attracted by the idea of spending your working life in academic publishing. Many people are involved in producing a book, the author(s), of course, designers, printers and so on, but the person who chooses what will be published is the Commissioning Editor.

Craig Fowlie is Commissioning Editor for books on Politics, International Relations and Asian Studies at Routledge:

'*95% of what we do is geared to the academic market. We try to produce books that will fit the courses currently on offer at universities in the UK and abroad. A lot of my job is finding out about courses and talking to academics to find out where the gaps in the market are. I go to academic conferences and do quite a lot of academic calling which means visiting university departments – in fact I've just come back from Singapore. Some work will come in unsolicited, but about 75% of my output – around 60 books a year – is commissioned, in other words I ask a specific academic to write a book on a particular subject.*'.

Before you can become a Commissioning Editor you have to learn the business which most people will do by working as an Editorial Assistant for a couple of years. Depending on the policy of the publishing house, the Assistant may or may not be involved in checking the original manuscript when it arrives from the author, proofreading the final product from the printers, writing the 'blurbs' for the covers and so on. However, wherever they work, all Assistants will provide the administrative back up to the project. They will chase up authors, arrange for the drawing up of contracts, contact the readers or referees (these are experts outside the publishing house who give their opinion on the content of the book), and liaise with other in-house departments such as production and marketing. So, if the Commissioning Editor is responsible for the content of the book, the Assistant is largely concerned with the process of producing the final product. As one Editorial Assistant at the Open University Press pointed out, 'students think publishing is going to be very creative and exciting, and that may be the case when you're higher up, but they must realise that as an Editorial Assistant there is a lot of admin. You have to be able to juggle different tasks because there will be a number of books going through at the same time and you also have to be very accurate with an eye for detail.'

Most Editorial Assistants, at least those who want to go on to become an Editor, will have a degree, though it does not have to be in the same subject as the books you work on. Craig Fowlie, for example, came from a background in English Literature and before becoming Commissioning Editor for politics worked on Routledge's Business and Economics lists. To strengthen your applications for jobs it can help to have done some work experience and there are also a number of courses on offer. The Publishers Association website www.publishing.org.uk contains a full listing of these. Vacancies are usually advertised in the quality press, particularly the *Guardian* and also the *Bookseller*. Starting salaries are around £14,000 to £17,000 and the minimum a new Commissioning Editor would expect to get is £20,000.

Teaching in Schools and Colleges

Schools: Until recently there were very few opportunities to teach politics or government in secondary schools. However, from September 2002 Citizenship will be added to the national curriculum in England and Wales for 11–16 year olds. According to the outline syllabus, it will cover:

- the legal and human rights and responsibility underpinning society, basic aspects of the criminal justic system and how both relate to young people

- the diversity of national, regional, religious and ethnic identities in the UK and the need for mutual respect and understanding

- central and local government, the public services they offer and how they are financed, and the opportunities to contribute

- the key characteristics of parliamentary and other forms of government

- the electoral system and the importance of voting

- the work of community-based, national and international voluntary groups

- the importance of resolving conflict fairly

- the significance of the media in society

- the world as a global community, and the political, economic, environmental and social implications of this, and the role of the European Union, the Commonwealth and the United Nations

The usual route for graduates to qualify as teachers is via a one-year full-time Postgraduate Certificate of Education (PGCE). About 20 institutions will be offering the PGCE in Citizenship, often combined with another subject, usually History. A searchable database of courses can be found on the website of the Graduate Teacher Training Registry (GTTR) at www.gttr.ac.uk.

Entry requirements for the course are a relevant degree plus English and Maths GCSE at minimum Grade C, or their equivalent. It is also useful to have some experience in a school. You can either arrange this yourself by contacting them direct, or there may be schemes operated by your university and your careers office should have details.

There are no tuition fees to pay and you will receive a training salary of £6,000 whilst on the course. The starting salary for new teachers is £16,038 (at April 2001). For more information on teaching as a career see www.canteach.org.uk and the National Union of Teachers website at www.nut.org.uk.

Further Education (FE) Colleges: 'A' level Government and Politics is frequently taught in FE colleges and there are also plans for Citizenship to be expanded into the post-16 sector. Although a teaching qualification is not a requirement to get a job initially, you will need to acquire a qualification within 2 years of starting work (if you are teaching full-time) and in any case, a PGCE might well help you to secure your first post. PGCE FE courses are offered at a handful of institutions in the country – details are on the GTTR website. Your fees will be paid and, at the moment, the £6,000 training salary applies. Unlike the situation for secondary teaching, however, it will be reviewed annually. PGCE secondary qualifications are also acceptable in FE colleges and they do give you the option of teaching in either setting.

Jobs are advertised in the *Guardian* and the *Times Educational Supplement*

Index

Academia 126–140, Summary 140–142
    Administration 131–133
    Entry Requirements 133–135
    External Activities 133
    Funding 135–137
    Job Market 138–139
    Research 129–131
    Teaching 127–129
    Terms & Conditions 139–140
Academic publishing, 210
Ambassador's Annual Reviews, 80
AMESS, David – Cons MP, 5
Amnesty International 147–148
ANDREWS–DEVINE, Kim – Labour Party
    Regional Organiser, 176–177
Arts & Humanities Research Board, 135

BBC, 189–191,193,201–206
BEAMISH, David – Clerk, House of Lords, 65–66
BEGG, Judith – Labour Party candidate, 7
BELL, Martin, OBE – Independent MP, 9, 201–206
Benefits Agency, 71
Bett Report, 126–127
Blair, Tony, 175, 176
Birmingham Post, 190
BORTHWICK, Bob – Senoir Lecturer in Politics,
    University of Leicester, 130–131
BRAZIER, Emma, House Reporter
BRERETON, Mike, Lecturer, 132
BROWN, Martin – Press & PR, Equity 182–183
BURNS, Patrick – Political Editior, BBC Midlands,
    189–190,193–194
BURRELL, Michael – Chair of Association of
    Professional Political Consultants 159

CABLE, Dr.Vincent – Lib.Dem MP, 5
Cabinet Office (Website), 209
Campbell, Alastair, 195
The Campaigner, 174
CANN, Elanor – Political Officer, Chemical
    Industries Association, 165–166
Central Office of Information, 160
Centre for Policy Studies, 144
Centre for Reform,144
Charter 88,148
Civil Service, 59,65, 73–101
    Decentralisation, 71
    Fast Stream Development Programme, 72–101
    General Fast stream 73–101, Summary: 99–101
        Applications 90–91
        Capita RAS (Employment agency),
            90,91,102, 111
        Clerkships in the Commons & Lords, 74
        Civil Service Selection Board (CSSB), 92
        CSSB diary, 93–98
        Diplomatic Service, 74, 78–82
        Entry requirements, 90
        European Fast Stream (EFS), 74, 75–78
        Home Civil Service, 73–74

        Positions & Salaries, 98
        Postings & Bidding for diplomatic service
            positions, 79
        Qualifying Test, 91
        Re-application, 99
        Recruitment, 72
        Successful applicants, 92–93
    Civil Service Main Stream 102–117
        Cabinet Office – graduate recruitment,
            107–110
        Executive Officer (B1), Summary, 109–110
            Salary & Rewards, 109
            Selection, 108–109
        Diplomatic Service – Operational Entry
            102–105, Summary, 106
        Recruitment and Selection, 105
        Foreign & Commonwealth Office (FCO) –
            Research Analyst, 110–112, Summary,112
        Selection & Promotion, 111–112
        Home Office, Research Staff – 113–115,
            Summary 115–117
        Placements, 114–115
        Other roles & views, 115
Civil Service Guide to Contacts with Lobbyists
    (1999), 158
CLEMO, Ida – Research Officer, GMB, 181
Clerks, 56– 68
    House of Commons / Clerks Dept, 56–67
        Assistant Clerk; Summary, 66–67
    Committee Office, 57
Committees; Select, 11, 57–60, 65, 113
Committee Reporters (Transcribers), 39–40
Confederation of British Industry (CBI), 149
Conservative Party, 170
Constituency Assistant, 19
COOPER, Kristiina – Political Correspondent
    194–195, 197

DALE, Iain – Managing Director, Politico's
    Bookshop, 9, 151–157
Daily Mail, 193
DEANS, John, Political Journalist, 193
Debates, 11
Demos, 144
Department for International Development, 76, 85
Department of Trade & Industry, 76,77
DHSS, 120–121
Dod's, 23, 27, 159–160
DUNCAN, Colin – Diplomatic service, 103–105
DUPRE, Darron – Research / Press Officer, TUC
    Wales, 182
DURRANT, Paul – News Editor, Eastern Daily
    Press, 192

EARL, John – Former Cons. Party Agent, 175–176
Early Day Motions (EDMs), 10
Eastern Daily Press, 192
Economic & Social Research Council, 135
Elections:1974, 30
    1979, 30
    1997, 5,12
    2001, 174
ENGEL, Natascha – Labour Trade Union Liason

Officer, 176–177
Enviroment Agency, 71
Equity Journal, 182
Erskine May, 36
European Free Trade Association, 78
European Union, 76, 78, 89

Fabian Society, 143
FABRE, Cecile LSE 132–133
FARRELLY, Paul – Labour MP, 4, 12
FCO 110–111
FLYNN, Paul, Labour MP, 39
Food Standards Agency, 83–84
FOSTER, Michael, 19
FOWLIE, Craig – Commissioning Editor,
    Routledges, 210–211
Friends of the Earth (FOE), 148
FROST, Chris – Senior Lecturer in Journalism,
    University of Central Lancs, 192
Further Education, 212–213

Gallup, 207–209
GARDNER, Lynn – Clerk of the Agricultural
    Committee, 57–60, 62
GEE, Helen – Cabinet Office, 107–108
Glasgow Herald, 54
Global Issues Research Group, 110
'The Government & Politics of Britain' – John P.
    Mackintosh, 187
GREEN, Dave – Research Officer, KFAT, 181–182
GREEN, Sarah – MEP PA, 20
GROCOTT, Bruce – MP, 28–34
Guardian, 23, 54, 62, 149, 163, 180, 191, 194, 209,
    213
GUNN, Janet – Head of Eastern Research Group,
    110–111
W.B. GURNEY and Sons, 43

HADLOW, Paul, Training Manager, *Hansard, 41*
HAMLYN, Matthew – Deputy Principal Clerk,
    Clerks Dept, 60–61
HAMMOND, Judicaelle – Ministry of Agriculture,
    Fish & Food (MAFF), 82–85
HEALY, Claire – Health Policy Officer, Labour
    Party, 172–173
HEBDITCH, Richard – Parliamentary &
    Campaigns Officer, NCVO, 163–165
Hansard, 36, 63, 159, 160, 193
Hollis, 165
House Magazine, 162
House of Commons, 9, 40, 74
House of Commons Order Paper, 159
House of Lords
    Hansard, 42–43
House of Lords Minutes of Proceedings, 160
House Reporters, 40–41

Independent Review of Higher Education Pay &
    Conditions, 1999, 126–127
Information & Research Staff, 48–56
Institute for Public Policy Research (IPPR), 144

JAMNEZHAD, Beatrice, Commons Library, 49

John Stuart Mill Institute, 144
Journalism, 189–198, Summary, 198–200
    The Lobby, 192–198
    Lobby Correspondents, 196–198
    Networking,196
    Parliamentary Press Gallery, 192–194
JUPP, Rachel – Researcher , Demos, 144–145

KAVANAGH, Trevor – Political Editor, the *Sun*,
    194, 198
KNIGHT, Alexa – Parliamentary Officer, Royal of
    Nursing, 166–168, 181

Labour Party, 143, 170, 172
National Executive Committee, 172
LAMBERT, Jean
LAURIE, Lee – Department for International
    Development, 12, 85–89
Learning Strategy Division, 108
Local Government & Quangos, 209–210
Local Government National Training Organisation,
    209
Lord's Weekly Agenda, 160
Library Clerk / Researcher 49–52
de LIMA, Natalie – Account Executive, Portcullis
    Research, 159–160

Market Research, 207–209
Media, 10, 31–31, 173–174
MEPs, 15
Millbank, 170, 176, 185
MILLER, Callum – European Fast Stream, 75–78
Ministry of Agriculture, Fisheries & Food, 78
Mirror Group, 190–191
MOOR, Helena – Campaign Assistant, 148
MORAN, Michael – Branch Organiser, NATFHE,
    179–181
MORI, 207–209
MPs, 4, 6–8
    Assembly Members, 15
    Attendance, 14
    Constituency, 9
    Constitutional Roles, 9
    Experience & Training, 6
    Pas, 27
    Parliamentary, 10
    Party Work, 12
    Promotion,14
    Salaries,14
    Second Employment, 6, 15
    Selection, 12
    Terms & Conditions, 14
    Useful Websites, 17
    Westminster, Summary, 16
    Work for Special Interests, 12
MSPs, 15

National Association of Teachers in Further &
    Higher Education (NATFHE), 139
National Farmer's Union, 82
New Statesman, 23, 25
NOP, 207–209
NTEKIM, Maniza – Policy Advisor, CBI, 149

Observer, 191, 193
O'CONNOR, Mike, CBE – Director Of
  Millennium Commission, 118–125
Official Reports (*Hansard*), 3639, Summary, 44–45
Open University Press, 211
Oxbridge, 93, 94, 105, 130

PA, Summary, 24–25
Parliamentary Assembly of the Council of Europe,
  57
Parliamentary Press Gallery, 192
Parliamentary On–Line Indexing Service (POLIS),
  49
Parliamentary Staff (Graduate positions), 35–66
Party Activity, 6–7
Party policy, 172
Party 'Staffers', 171–172
PAXTON, Will – Research Assistant, 144
PAYNE, Margeret, Parliamentray Assistant, 19
PEACOCK, Julie, Journalist, Radio Stoke, 189
People, 191
PETCH, Eleanor – Diplomatic Service, 78–82, 102
PGCE, 212–213
Policy Studies Institute (PSI), 144
Political Parties & Trade Unions, 170–184
    Conservative, 170
        Campaigns & Elections, 174
    Entry, 183
    Green, 171
    Labour, 170, 172
        National Executive Committee, 172
    Liberal Democrat, 170,171
    Media & Communications, 173–174
    Political Party Worker, Summary, 177–178
    Research, Political / Parliamentary &
    Press Officers, 181–183
Politician's Staff, 18–27
    Constituency Assistant, 19
    Examples of, 19–22
    Executive Secretary / PA, 18
    Getting in, 23
    Parliamentary Assistant, 18
    Promotion, 24
    Research Assistant, 19
    Skills, Qualities & Background, 22
    Special Advisors ('Policy Wonks' & 'Spin
    Doctors'), 25–27
    Terms, Conditions & Salaries, 23–24
Politico's, 151–157
Post–graduate & PhD, 128, 129, 133–135
PRESCOTT, John, 175
Press Association News Traineeship Programme, 191
Press Office, 173
Pressure Groups, 146–150
Public Affairs (Lobbying), 158–168, Summary,
  168–169
    Entry & Salaries, 162–163
    In–house Public Affairs, 163–167
    Political Consultancy, 160–163
    Political Monitoring, 159–160
    Skills & Qualities, 168

Quality Assurance Agency (QAA), 132

Quangos, 158, 159, 161, 209–210
Question Time
    PMQs, 10
    House of Lords, 7
Research Assessment Exercise (RAE), 130
Research Development & Statistics Directorate
  (RDS), 113
RODGER, Alan – Press Research Officer, Scottish
  Conservative Office, 174
ROSE, Catherine – Senior Account Executive,
  GJW BSMG Worldwide, 161–162
ROSEN, Greg – Research Officer / Political
  Consultant, 185–188
ROSS, Graham – Scottish Parliamentary Clerk,
  53–54
Routledge, 210
Royal Institute of International Affairs (RIIA), 77,
  144

SARKAR, Simon – Gallup, 208
Scotsman, 54
SEATON, Janet, 53
Select Committees, 57–60, 65, 133
SHARPE, Jacqy – Principle Clerk, Select
  Committee, 59
Short, Clare, 19
SMALL, Karen – PhD student, 137–138
SMITH, Katie – Environment, Transport &
  Regional Affairs Select Committee Specialist,
  61–63
Speaker, 60
SPENCER–CHAPMAN, Kathleen – MEP PA, 21
Standing Committees, 57
STENNING, Anna – Amnesty International
  London Press Officer, 147
Strength Finder On Line Applications, 208
SUTHERLAND, Lorraine, Deputy Editor, *Hansard*,
  40

Table Office, 56
    Early Day Motions, 56
    Future Business, 56
Order of Business / Order Paper, 56, 63
TAYLOR, Dr. Richard, 6
Teaching, 211–213
Think Tanks & Pressure Groups, 143–146
    Researcher / Assistant, 144–146, Summary, 146
    Entry,145
    Further employment, 145–146
    Skills for working in, 145

THORP, Arabella – House of Commons Library
  Clerk, 50–52
Times, The, 193
    Educational Supplement, 213
Trade Unions, 178–183, Summary, 183–184
    Branch Organisers, 179–181
Trade Union Congress (TUC), 149, 179, 181–182,
  187
TUC Organisational Academy Training Scheme,
  179–181

UK Press & Public Relations Annual, 160

Vote Bundle, 159

WARD, Rachel – GMTV,194, 195,196
WEBBER, Araba – Local Groups Officer, Charter
  88, 148–149
Weekly Information Bulletin, 160
Westminster, 35
  Working in / Travel to from, 14
WHEWAY, Jude, Committee Reporter
Whips, 14
WHITE, Michael – Political Editor, the *Guardian*,
  194
WOOD, Edward, Commons Library, 51
World Trade Organisation (WTO), 76, 77, 89

ZIMMECK, Meta – Head of Community
  Research, Home Office 113–114